RUNNING
FROM
GRACE,
CAUGHT
BY
MERCY

—— John M. Benevides ——

ISBN 978-1-63874-688-1 (paperback)
ISBN 978-1-63874-689-8 (digital)

Christian Faith Publishing, Inc.
832 Park Avenue
Meadville, PA 16335
www.christianfaithpublishing.com

Printed in the United States of America

This book is dedicated to my beautiful wife, Kathleen, my best friend, my comforter, and my bride for life, because she lived through my hell. Her honesty and loving and caring spirit should be an inspiration to all of us. There are not enough words to thank my brothers and sisters in the body of Christ for how you have helped me with my walk with the Lord.

CONTENTS

PREFACE

After wandering through the sinful wilderness for most of my life, I humbly accepted Jesus Christ as my personal Savior and received His salvation through *my desperation*. I had been told that I had an addict's personality and can testify that I have spent the majority of my life suffering from various types of substance abuse. Through personal examples and carnal living, it is my hope to show you how the Lord took a broken soul and transformed me into a child of God.

It is my opinion that I was the worst type of addict, and allow me to explain why. I was not homeless, a beggar, or what your mind's eye imagines. I was a father, a husband, a business owner, a friend, a productive member of society, and the guy sitting next to you in church, a theater, or a restaurant.

This autobiography is brutally honest and transparent to a fault. The stories that are shared are G-rated and only a small fraction of the events of my life. The primary reason for writing this book is not to embarrass myself but to glorify God, our Creator, our Redeemer, our Savior, and my Friend. We need to appreciate that no matter what we have done or failed to do in our lives, we are never too far from God's love and grace.

I have felt the thickness and glory of God on more than one occasion and can testify that it is complete joy, and nothing in this world can compare. It can be difficult to understand or really appreciate the statement *"the flesh versus the Spirit,"* but every thought and action we do is controlled by one or the other. **"For the flesh lusts against the Spirit, and the Spirit against the flesh; and these are contrary to one another, so that you do not do the things that you wish" (Galatians 5:17).**

You may notice that several of the beginning chapters refer to myself as the corruptible seed, which is the corruptible seed of Adam, the fall of mankind, or however you see it. The second half of my story is what God has done in my life since I surrendered myself to Him. I have included Bible verses throughout the book, which I believe is pertinent to my life at that moment in time. All verses are from the NKJV.

My carnal mind would like to believe that I have dedicated my life to Christ, but any of us who truly believe this may be deceiving ourselves, unless you are living in a developing country and/or doing full-time mission work. Please do not misunderstand me. Doing what we can is better than doing nothing at all, but I think we throw around the term that we have devoted our life to Christ without any real merit. You may believe that statement is my opinion, but how do we measure up against the Apostle Paul? **"From the Jews five times I received 40 strips minus one. Three times I was beaten with rods; once I was stoned; three times I was shipwrecked; a night and a day I have been in the deep" (2 Corinthians 11:24–25).**

I have always felt good when donating my time and efforts for others, but when I read about a twelve-year-old boy from Detroit who started making lunches for the homeless, and his efforts is now a multimillion-dollar food bank, my efforts seem to fall short. Allow me to babble.

The Gospel has not changed in two thousand years, and when Jesus told the original apostles to spread the news to the corners of the earth, He did not say after you have become educated, wealthy, married, a parent, or comfortable. In fact, he told one of His followers not to return home to say goodbye to his father; remember, allow the dead to bury the dead.

I know my thoughts are borderline legalistic, but honestly, don't you think that mankind has watered down the Gospel to fit our current lifestyle? I will not dwell on this, but sit down and figure out how many hours of the 168 hours per week you spend with or serving God. Most of us might be at 10 percent, if we are lucky. Whether you are a new believer, a nonbeliever, or a seasoned Christian, I believe you will find this book worth your time.

ACKNOWLEDGMENTS

I am still a work in progress and owe everything to God. **"For there are three who bear witness in heaven; the Father, the Word and the Holy Spirit; and these three are one" (1 John 5:7).** I have been blessed beyond measure and would humbly like to thank God for His unending love, grace, and mercy. I also ask that He would continue to bless us, individually and also corporately, with the following prayer.

I pray to You, Heavenly Father, that everyone who reads this will find the peace, joy, and wisdom that can only be found with/in/through You. We ask that You reveal Yourself to all that call Your name in the way that only You are capable of doing, with and without our knowledge.

Help us to understand and appreciate Your kingdom and the glory that awaits us and not to worry about the trivial events of this life. Allow us the resources and boldness to gracefully speak the Gospel to the unsaved, in Jesus's glorious name. Amen.

CHAPTER 1

Hitting the Wall

It is December 2010 in beautiful South Florida. The weather is perfect, and the snowbirds are migrating south. The waves have been worth waiting for, and living in the golf capital of the world certainly is a blessing.

My wife and I have teenage twins named Johnny and Megan, and we live in a beautiful home near the beach. I have three older children named Kevin, Kristy, and Renee from a prior marriage, and they live close by. Having a stepparent and an ex-wife when children are involved can be a challenge, to say the least.

My wife and the children are healthy and appear happy. What more could you want? Loving and protecting my family used to be the only thing that mattered. **"The thief comes to steal, kill and destroy. I have come that they may have life, and that they may have it more abundantly" (John 10:10).**

The reality of my life and my addiction to pain pills are beginning to take its toll on me, again. Do you realize how difficult it is to eat hundreds of opiates on a monthly basis and still try to be a productive member of society?

What originated as prescribed pain medication for several physical issues has now left me doctor shopping, visiting "pill mills," trading narcotics, and doing illegal street buys. Is this the man Christ died for, or have I allowed Satan to control my soul? Truthfully, I know the latter to be true.

I am currently working the night shift throwing newspapers because I can no longer work as a private investigator due to my dependency on narcotics. Having to now perform physical labor has increased my consumption of pills regardless of my personal efforts.

One evening before work, I drove to the beach, rolled a fatty, and began to think about my life and how I had become consumed by the drugs and the hamster wheel of being an addict. I began thinking about the dozens of people I had disappointed in my life and my frequent thoughts of suicide. After getting stoned, I reminded myself that you only get out of life what you put into it.

Christmas was just a few days away, and I can't help but think that it will not be a joyous time for us. Christmas has always been a magical time to me, but because of my substance abuse and bad attitude, I find myself being withdrawn from my family, friends, and people in general.

I used to look forward to buying my children and friends presents and have often been criticized that I did too much for too many. I remember years ago when the kids were younger, there were so many presents under our tree that our living room was a sea of wrapping paper. As I look at our tree today, I only see three presents which are not even for my children. I gave them cash in a plain white envelope. I consider most of the other holidays just a reason to party and try to fill that empty void in my soul. Was Halloween started by a demonic dentist? Just a thought.

The tension between my wife and I was getting red lined. She knows the easiest way to avoid conflict is to ignore the problem, which is me. After a heated discussion, we decided that it would be best for the children for me not to be at the house right now.

I personally thought that this was my opportunity to decide if I wanted to continue living among the dead. **"Let the dead bury the dead" (Matthew 8:32)**. Looking back, I should have entered a professional facility and received the treatment that was needed, but I seem to always do things the hard way.

Through God's grace and provisions, money is currently not an issue because I am very good at my job. I had spent the prior twelve months providing a level of service to my customers that they had not experienced before. As a result of my due diligence, I received over ten thousand dollars in Christmas tips.

Not wanting to permanently abandon my family, I decided that I would have one hell of a New Year's celebration, even if it was just me. I purchased an ounce of "skunk bud," a large amount of cocaine, a carton of cigarettes and cashed in more paper for the three narcotics. I checked into an expensive local hotel and paid ten nights in advance and secured five hundred for room service.

As I was getting settled into my room, I smoked a huge blunt and snorted several lines of cocaine and decided not to go to work. After working over six hundred consecutive days, I just quit, without even a phone call. There were another dozen people I disappointed.

I spent the next week doing the most drugs that I had ever consumed at one time and, quite honestly, was trying to escape the pressures and responsibilities of life. I found myself once again thinking about suicide and which method would be suitable for a spineless coward. I have to believe that anyone who seriously considers taking their own life does so without planning and/or really considering the physical act.

I understand rage and how it can lead to death, but planning your own death? My mindset was that I had hundreds of reasons for dying, but the embarrassment that this would cause my family was the only reason for living, or so I thought. I seriously considered every physical type of suicide.

After close to two weeks, I returned to the house, and I became severely depressed, mostly because of quitting my job and my continued addiction. Suicide appeared to be my only option, regardless of those left in the wake of my evil. I had narrowed it down to a drug overdose or electrocution. I began thinking, *Should I write one note for everyone or write individual notes?* The when and the where to kill yourself seemed very important.

Who would find the body? Could I make it look like an accident? These thoughts stayed with me for the next several days as I continued my daily routine of being consumed by thoughts and actions all revolving around the narcotics. *How many more do I have? How many have I taken today? Has it been enough days to get a refill yet? What store this week?*

God's wake-up call for me finally resonated at a pharmacy that I had never visited before. As I approached the counter, the pharmacist looked at me, shook his head with disgust, and said, "Let me guess, Oxys or Xanax?"

Through God's wisdom and grace, I have learned that if we just pay attention to our surroundings, God uses people every day to guide us through life. **"A man's heart plans his ways, but the Lord directs his steps" (Proverbs 16:9).** A sad reality was that I was holding paper for each of these narcotics and that my physical appearance was that evident.

I returned to my car and sat there for close to two hours thinking about what had just happened. I looked at myself in the mirror, and quite honestly, it scared me to death. Because of the drugs, I was missing several teeth, and the ones that remained were discolored and nasty. My son Johnny always said that I looked like a well-dressed homeless man.

In my heart, I knew that I had to get clean, but having been addicted to opiates for over five years and other vices for forty, I began to wonder, *Could I quit?* My first thought was, *No way!* I seldom go a few hours without taking a pill or smoking a joint.

What happened next was the loving and caring hand of God and His endless mercy. I began thinking about all of the children in hospitals with cancer fighting to live, and all I wanted was my life to end. The only way I can explain my feelings is that my selfish flesh wanted to end it all, but my spirit wanted me to surrender.

Suddenly, I remembered *eternity*! I had been so medicated from the narcotics that I did not consider eternity while thinking about suicide. Then God put this on my heart: *You think you are miserable now? Eternity is forever.* I have never doubted anything that I learned about God. I was just too disobedient to really care. How can you honor and love someone you can't see? I have enough trouble loving those that I can see.

The long difficult road to recovery is started by taking the first step, and like everything else, it begins in your mind and, hopefully, in your heart as well. I decided to try and get off the Oxys and told my wife that I wanted to rejoin the living and asked her to pray for me.

I have always been a numbers guy, and I guess that is why I figured out that during the last five-plus years, I had taken close to twenty thousand pills! I suspect that my liver is the size of an olive. I realized that food would be a problem, so staying hydrated might be the difference between living and dying.

In my mind, even if I died, at least I was trying to do what I thought was right, and that should mean something to God. You know, like people who believe they will see the Prince of Peace if they are just nice to other people. **"I am the way, the truth and the life. No one comes to the Father except through me" (John 14:6).**

The first evening, I remember pacing the floor for hours at a time and trying to lay down and watch TV to take my mind off of what was happening. I may have slept ten minutes the entire time. When I saw the sun come up on Saturday, I knew that I was in for the fight of my life.

Johnny and Megan were starting their first job this morning at the local market where my wife works her second job. When they left the house, I honestly wondered if I would ever see them again.

I was lying in bed with several Gatorade bottles, a bucket for the evil in my body, and a rosary and crucifix. I asked God to forgive my sins, confessed that Jesus Christ was the Savior of the world, and begged Him to help me. I prayed that He would restore me to a man that he could use and just make me new. I was completely humbled, broken, and a shell of a man. **"My grace is sufficient for you, for My strength is made perfect in your weakness" (2 Corinthians 12:9).**

I have seen dozens of people accepting Christ at altar calls and revivals, but this was not immediate or life changing, which I contribute to my state of mind and the amount of narcotics still in my system. During the next few days, I watched every religious program on TV and would not release the cross in my hand. The third and fourth days were usually the worst, and I remember crying out over and over for Jesus to help me, but the narcotics and demonic influences were still winning. **"Then they will seek my face: in their affliction they will earnestly seek me" (Hosea 5:15).**

The biggest problem with detox is not the headaches, the weakness, the terrible feeling in your stomach, the body aches, the chills and hot flashes, or the loss of appetite; it is the inability to sleep. The best you can hope for is napping a few minutes every several hours.

I could feel the presence of evil and found myself saying prayers for hours at a time in efforts to defeat the evil one. There were times that an extremely strong presence was just telling me to end it all. Although I didn't know it, I was experiencing the battle of the flesh versus the spirit.

I had only slept a few hours in four days. I knew that I had to sleep, or I wasn't going to make it. I prayed the best prayer that I knew from my heart and asked Him to please help me as I took about a dozen Xanax. My mindset was that I would either get some sleep or die trying.

I remember thinking about how I had been given everything in this world to be successful, but I got off track somewhere. Why did I allow my selfishness and sinful nature to ruin my life? Whether it was the narcotics or the healing power of Jesus Christ or both (only God knows), I entered what I can only describe as a spiritual coma.

The next few days, I slipped in and out of consciousness, thinking about my earthly sins and about my life in general. I recalled people and events that I had not thought about in years which I would like to share.

CHAPTER 2

The Corruptible Seed Is Planted

I began thinking about my early childhood when I lived up north before moving to South Florida when I was six. I grew up in a loving home, and my parents insisted that my brother and I attend church every Sunday, even though they were always too busy. My opinion is that children learn more from examples of action and not just words.

I made the mistake of questioning my parents once why they didn't go to church or read the Bible. My parents were old school, and their decisions were not to be questioned. This was back in the day when parents physically disciplined their children, and we were taught to be seen and not heard!

My mother was Italian, and my father was Portuguese. The best visual example I can give you of them are Frank and Marie from the sitcom *Everybody Loves Raymond*. The similarities between my mom and the character Marie are freaky weird, from the clothes she wore, her attitude, how she cooked, how she controlled the house, and how she coddled her youngest, which was me.

My father entered the military at sixteen because he wanted to serve in World War II. He was someone who seldom showed any emotion, and I don't remember him ever telling me that he loved me, even though I knew he did. He had a big heart but just did not know how to show his love without being considered weak. Generational curse or just human nature?

My mother was ten years older than my father, and her first husband was killed in front of her while changing a flat tire. His name was Leo, and he was Jewish, which did not go over well with the old-school Italian family. Leo being called home in the prime of his life certainly is sad, but would I have ever been born if this did not happen? Would any of my children or grandchildren have been born?

> **Blessed be the God and Father of our Lord Jesus Christ, who has blessed us with every spiritual blessing in the heavenly places in Christ, just as He chose us in Him before the foundation of the world, that we should be holy and without blame before Him in love, having predestined us to adoption as sons by Jesus Christ to Himself, according to the good pleasure of His will. (Ephesians 1:3–5)**

My parents were the hardest workers that I knew. My father worked a full-time job and also had several side jobs. My mother worked forty-plus hours per week at her job, shopped and cleaned every Saturday, and cooked the week's meals on Sunday.

One of my fondest childhood memories was coming home on a Sunday afternoon after playing ball all day and seeing all that food. Eggplant and chicken parmesan, chicken or veal cutlets, two dozen meatballs and sausage floating in gallons of sauce, several pounds of pasta and pepperoni or sausage bread makes you hungry, huh? Get something to eat; I'll wait.

I owe everything I learned about cooking to my mother and will assume from her mother. My grandmother died when I was five years old and was my only grandparent still living when I was born. My mother was forty when I was born, and I was always self-conscious about her age because she was close to the age of most of my friend's grandparents.

I have always been amazed how society changes the rules and laws, and what is acceptable or unacceptable today may not be tomorrow. Even as a young child, I knew something was not right when you are riding in a three-ton vehicle without seat belts, with a can of gasoline in the trunk, all the windows up and no air conditioning, and both your parents smoking.

I started smoking cigarettes when I was ten years old and only recently quit after smoking for fifty years. You parents who smoke in front of your kids should be concerned; not trying to be legalistic, just speaking from experience.

I want to share something that happened when I was eleven or twelve, and my older brother Ricky was fourteen. I was lying down on a sofa reading a comic book, and my brother removed the metal darts from the dartboard which was on the wall over my head. He told me to move several times, but I insisted that I was there first. You know how kids are. He acted like he was ready to release a Bob Gibson fastball and followed through.

I remember saying "I knew you wouldn't do it" and laughed, until I saw the look on his face. I looked up and saw the feather from the end of the dart which was sticking in the middle of my forehead. I freaked out, and after he pulled the dart out, it never even bled; there was just a pinhole in my head. A couple inches to either side, and I would have been blinded for life.

My brother outweighed me by over a hundred pounds, so hand-to-hand combat was not an option. I went into my bedroom and grabbed one of the old wooden clothes hangers and threw it as hard as I could at his face. It hit him above his left eye, and blood was everywhere.

My aunt brought him to the emergency room, and twenty-two stitches later, he came home. I had no remorse or regrets, an eye for an eye literally, until my mom got home and took out the oversize wooden spoon. We never played darts again, and he always had a hidden fear of me after that afternoon. Honestly, I am not that bad; I just got tired of putting up with the things that older brothers do!

I started dating before I was a teenager and remember being at parties while in the fifth and sixth grades, playing spin the bottle, post office, and seven minutes in heaven. I don't know if the parents were that naïve, or perhaps they were just drinking and smoking. It was the late sixties. I had sexual relations before I reached middle school.

Everything started to go south when I was in the eighth grade in the early seventies. My first social introduction to substance abuse was in shop class. I walked into the restroom to see a kid from my neighborhood huffing paint thinner from a paper towel. Everything my parents tried to teach me about drugs went out the window, mostly because of trying to be cool and peer pressure. **"Watch and pray, lest you enter into temptation. The spirit indeed is willing, but the flesh is weak" (Matthew 26:41).** I would like to tell you that I didn't get involved with huffing, but I did.

I had always been a hard worker and earned money throwing newspapers and cutting two dozen lawns in my neighborhood. In the early seventies, I was earning one hundred dollars per week which is equal to about a thousand a week in today's money. Try to appreciate what things cost back then.

My parents' mortgage was $70 dollars a month. A brand-new Corvette was about five grand. Gasoline was $0.45 a gallon, cigarettes were $0.40 a pack, milk was under a dollar, and bread was $0.20 a loaf. An ounce of marijuana was $20 dollars and now sells for about $400–$600, depending on where you live and your personal preference.

The reason I mention the money is because I had been saving for years, and think I had several thousand dollars saved which was about to change. I was first introduced to marijuana as a young teenager and absolutely loved it. Would my life have turned out differently if I had never started taking drugs and parlayed that savings account? **"Where your treasure is, there will your heart be also" (Matthew 6:21).**

I bought my first motorcycle at fifteen which gave me freedom and liberty to do what I wanted. It's funny how your friends are not around when you don't have what they want, kind of like my relationship with God at that time in my life. **"Wealth makes many friends, but the poor is separated from his friend" (Proverbs 19:4).**

By my sophomore year in high school, I was completely controlled by girls and drugs. My hair was long, and the tension in

America was redlined due to racism, equal rights, the military, and the Vietnam War. During the last ten years as a country, John F. Kennedy, Robert Kennedy, and Dr. Martin Luther King Jr. were killed in cold blood, and our imports exceeded our exports.

I would like to share with you a few things that my friends and I did on a fairly regular basis. There was a motor speedway west of town that was in need of repairs and was usually closed during the week. We would go there late at night, climb the fifty- to sixty-feet observation/camera tower and sit there for hours and drink and smoke out. How we ever made it down the ladder is another one of His blessings that we forget about.

We frequently visited Juno Beach and hung out at a place coined double roads, a shell rock road that ran adjacent to the ocean and A1A. Dozens of us would listen to jams, enjoy the ocean breeze, and drink and smoke out. Most of the patrolling officers usually looked the other way as long as we were cool and not too loud.

I began using cocaine, THC, acid, and mushrooms on a fairly regular basis. I became consumed by drugs and, even though I continued to work, the majority of my money went to partying. When my money ran out, I stole from my parents, my brother, friends, and even did some B and Es. My parents must have stayed up all night worrying. Did I fail to mention that my father was a police officer? His friends and associates kept me out of jail more than once.

My brother was the complete opposite of me; he was serious about school and even more serious about his relationship with Jesus Christ. He was what we called a Jesus freak and tried to enlighten me numerous times about the Gospel and the glory of God, but the veil was still covering my eyes and heart. **"But even to this day, when Moses is read, a veil lies on their heart" (2 Corinthians 3:15).**

My girlfriend and I and another couple were joyriding one Sunday in my father's old beater in an open field which seemed harmless enough, until I saw a half a dozen deputies driving at a high rate of speed in my direction. The open field was actually the county's runway and was private property. I received several traffic citations and was allowed to leave, even though we had an open bottle of Vodka and we were underage. I suspect that the officers knew my father, although they never asked about him.

Several months later, I had to attend court, and I had never told my parents about the tickets. My father was working the third shift, so when he fell asleep, I stole his keys and drove myself to the courthouse. I had lost driving privileges for something else I must have done, and my bike was in need of repairs.

When the judge fined me $350 plus court costs, I came close to losing it. That may not seem extreme to you, but that fine was equal to about $3,000 dollars in today's money. The judge was trying to make an example of the sixteen-year-old long-haired punk.

I told the judge that I didn't have that kind of money, and he asked if my parents would bring it. Realizing that I was facing 30–60 days in juvenile hall if I said no, my answer was "absolutely." He asked the bailiff to bring me to the holding cell and have me call my parents. Oh yeah, I stole my dad's car, and he was still sleeping. That call was very unpleasant, and he made good on the threats he said on the phone when he showed up four hours later.

Now here's the crazy part. When they brought me into a room for processing, the bailiff told them that a strip search was not necessary because my father, who was a police officer, was bringing the court the fine. That was when I remembered I had a few grams of hash and a one-hitter pipe in my boot, which seems insane, but my dad's vehicle did not lock.

They placed me in a holding cell with a biker who looked like Bob Segger. He told me he had been there for over two days and was waiting to be transported to North Florida and was surprised that they put me in with him. I told him my story and asked him if he wanted to smoke some hash. He asked me if I was Jesus. We carefully smoked, and an hour later, they brought us green bologna sandwiches and Kool-Aid. I had to stop telling this story because even my closest friends wouldn't believe me.

During our time together, my girlfriend and I were sexually active, and she got pregnant when we were sixteen or seventeen. Both our parents knew that we were not ready to raise a child, so abortion seemed to be our only option. I am not trying to place blame and guilt elsewhere, but why didn't someone suggest adoption or something other than murder? I was only a kid; I didn't know what I was doing.

She was 16-17 weeks along when we went to the clinic, and her mother physically assaulted me when she came outside after the procedure. This would have been her first grandchild. This is a regret I still have, but God's grace and mercy covers it all. **"There is therefore now no condemnation to those who are in Christ Jesus, who do not walk according to the flesh, but according to the spirit" (Romans 8:1).**

I call her Grace (getting what you don't deserve), and she is forty-plus years old now and waiting to see me when He calls me home. My girlfriend and I continued dating, but because of our shame and guilt, things were never the same.

In June of '73, I heard that four of my friends from school were in a very serious car accident after surfing. They all sustained serious injuries, but one of my best friends had received a spinal cord injury and was told he would never walk again.

He was in the ICU, and walking into his room was one of the most surreal feelings that I have ever felt. He was lying on his back on a rotating bed, with two bolts drilled into his skull supporting a heavy sandbag. I was told not to show emotion when I saw him, which was extremely difficult.

He was freaked out because a few days earlier, he was surfing and had a promising career as a singer. During the next several weeks, I tried to visit him every day because I cared about him, and after the first week, most people stopped going to visit. After numerous months of pure survival, he spent the next several years in hospitals in North Florida and Georgia.

Some of these details are a bit vague because this is one of the times during the seventies that I have memory loss. I do know that he went through hell for several years, and his determination, perseverance, and God's will allowed him to walk years later with the use of crutches.

Within a few years, he got married, moved to Hollywood, and has become a very successful writer for numerous sitcoms and movies. I continued partying and never returned to school after the summer. My parents tried to tell me the importance of an education, but I refused to listen.

CHAPTER 3

The Corruptible Seed Takes Root

I literally spent the majority of my time being a concert freak and worked part time at various jobs so I could afford smoke and partying. I would like to share one concert that we attended at the motor speedway that I mentioned earlier. They had planned an outdoor festival with the headliner being Eric Clapton.

Shortly after our arrival, God opened the skies with one of the famous sideway rains that frequently occur in the summer in South Florida. Within a few hours, there were twenty to thirty thousand people sitting in mud up to our waists, and we decided it was a good time to take the acid that we had brought.

A few hours before Eric was scheduled to take the stage, a fifty- to sixty-miles-per-hour wind and the hardest rain that I have ever endured blew all the speakers off of the platform and the roof off of the stage. A few minutes later, they said that they were going to have to cancel the concert. Yeah, that went over well. We had been sitting in mud for hours, and most of us idolized Eric. Before things got out of hand, they told us it would be several hours before they could reconstruct the roof and replace the sound system. Eric finally took the stage and was amazing. A few of us wondered if he would open with "Let It Rain." I later read that Eric was suffering from heroin addiction at this time in his life.

During the summer of '76, I began to grow tired of my ways. After obtaining my high school GED, I was hired by a major grocery store chain bagging groceries or, as we liked to say, a packaging engineer. I truly enjoyed having steady employment and some purpose in my life. **"For I know the thoughts that I think towards you, says the Lord, thoughts of peace and not of evil, to give you a future and a hope" (Jeremiah 29:11).** Within a year, I was transferred to the grocery department and began climbing the corporate ladder and investing a large portion of my salary in their company stocks.

I was sharing an apartment with a buddy from work, and we would usually go back to the homestead and drink and smoke out. One particular evening while playing cards, I won a few hundred dollars from my boss, and he wasn't happy. I told him not to worry about it; he was my boss. He must have felt convicted because an hour later, he made a strange proposal. I am not proud of what happened next, but remember I was only nineteen and the corruptible seed of Adam. He had the keys to the grocery store and told me I could have three minutes in the store to get whatever I wanted, if that would settle the debt. I was an usually fast runner and grabbed about five hundred dollars of the finest meats and seafood, and we ate well for several weeks.

In 1977, I began dating a girl whom I had known from high school and thought that I was in love with. Let's call her Sue. I was also seeing Grace's mother on the side and another girl I knew from California when she was in town. Trying to keep all the lies straight became near impossible, and when the three of them showed up at my apartment one afternoon, they told me to make a decision which one I wanted to date.

Within a year, I married Sue at the young age of twenty. Looking back, I suppose I got married because several of my closest friends did, and I was excited about the thought of playing house and a honeymoon. I had witnessed and participated in several weddings but never understood being joined together in God's house and receiving His blessing and the importance of being one. **"Therefore a man shall leave his father and mother and be joined to his wife, and they shall become one flesh" (Genesis 2:24).**

Needless to say, I did not take the sacred bond of marriage seriously and have only recently learned that marriage is an example of

Christ and His church. Shortly after we were married, I quit my job because of a conflict, even though I was now in management. This selfish nature of mine has followed me throughout my adult life.

Because of this selfishness, Sue and I had a huge fight, and after she left for work, I did what any immature, drug-oriented fool would do; I withdrew several hundred dollars from our account, got drunk, and drove to Miami International Airport and flew to Jamaica. I had never been on an airplane or out of the United States, and my first day on the island was spent with an unknown local that I had met at the local watering hole.

I told him I wanted to get some smoke, and after convincing him I was not with the DEA, I was on his scooter being escorted to the mountains. We then walked about a half mile into the steep hillside, and I honestly began fearing for my life. No one knew where I was.

He took me to a shack where a Rastafarian lived, and when I saw ounces of weed stacked up like cords of wood against the wall, I became excited. He asked me how much I wanted to buy, and I told him a half pound if the price was right. We settled on one hundred American dollars. And I always thought I could smoke with the best of them, until he twisted up a one-fourth ounce and laced it with hash oil; I choked like a rookie. I was so stoned that when he dropped me off at my room, I never left until I had to go to the airport two days later.

When I returned home, I tried to make things right, but a leopard can't change his spots just because he wants to. I agreed to try and change, but within a few weeks, she told me that she was going to stay with her parents for a while to decide what she wanted to do.

During the Fourth of July weekend, I attended a party at the beach with some friends that morning and began drinking early and having a pity party when I got home. I called my wife who told me that she already had plans for later in the day, which infuriated me. Feeling rejected, I called my gal pal in California and told her what was going on in my life. She suggested that I come out for a long holiday weekend and booked me a flight. By the late afternoon, I was once again driving south to the Miami airport, drunk.

It was nice to see her again, and we enjoyed the La Jolla neighborhoods and all that Cali has to offer. Have you ever been involved with someone who likes you much more than you like them? I did not even consider that I had committed adultery because I was still legally married. I disappointed my employer and friend when I returned home two days late.

Within a few days, one of my wife's best friends stopped by and asked me to meet her later that evening at a restaurant at the beach. When I asked why, she said that Sue wanted her to talk and relay her thoughts to me.

I will not bore you with the details, but while meeting with her later that evening, Sue and her family removed all of the possessions from the apartment. When I returned home, I was not happy, to say the least.

This was the first time I remember thinking about suicide, and I became severely depressed and withdrawn. I purchased several of those automatic bug bombs and went into an extremely small closet and set the bombs off. Much to my surprise, I woke up several hours later with the most intense headache I have ever had. On a positive note, I never had a pest problem again!

The following weekend, I was at a restaurant near the beach and saw a friend that used to date one of my best friends. She told me that she had recently been in an abusive relationship and had just left and had nowhere to stay. I told her about my marriage situation and offered my floor and a sleeping bag for her. We had not planned on it, but after drinking that evening, we were intimate, and I had once again committed adultery. Alcohol has a way of helping you make poor decisions.

The following morning, she had taken a shower and was sitting in the living room with a towel around her and wet hair as I went in to take my shower. When I got out, she told me that some girl had stopped by to see me, but she told her that I was still in the shower. It was my wife!

I later heard that she showed up to apologize about taking all of the furniture and being so sneaky. By mid-August, I was served my walking papers which I certainly deserved. I asked my friend to make other living arrangements.

Remember earlier when I said that I have never been a good financial steward? Well, those stocks that I had purchased were now worth about five grand, and I knew it was time for changes in latitudes and changes in attitudes. I sold all of my stocks and most of my personal belongings, financed a newer car, and headed west. I ended up in Pueblo, Colorado, and visited one of my closest friends from high school named Mike.

I had known Mike since the early seventies, and we once traveled from South Florida to Centerville, Iowa, in a Greyhound Bus which was fifty-one hours. He had recently been married, and the three of us traveled extensively throughout the state.

After a few weeks, we said goodbye, and I spent the next several weeks in Utah, Vegas, Arizona, and I decided to visit my gal pal in San Diego. She was in a relationship at the time, and my visit was short and not so sweet. I found it funny how it was fine for her to spend time with me just a few months ago when I was married but not okay when she was dating. Mankind will always disappoint you.

I remember sitting in hotel rooms thinking that I should just start over and find a nice quiet place to plant new roots. I also remember driving further and further East until I hit the Florida state line. I returned to my parents' house, which certainly was an adjustment after being on your own.

I found a job as a server at a high-end restaurant and told them I had several years' experience, even though I had only worked as a dishwasher at a few diners. How hard could it be? I have eaten at hundreds of restaurants.

To this day, I have an enormous amount of respect for anyone working in the food service industry. People are very difficult, to say the least. I remained at the restaurant for close to a year and also worked full time for the bottled water company in efforts to save money and get back on my feet. My substance abuse escalated because all I did was party and work, and the restaurant business encourages this type of lifestyle.

I remained in contact with Mike and in September of '81, I decided to move to Colorado and eventually found a job at a Best Western Hotel and Restaurant. I worked as a server, and after a few weeks, I worked out a deal with the manager where I began living at the hotel in one of the older rooms. I provided a security presence and was given the keys to the bar and restaurant, which I tried not to abuse but...

I continued working at the hotel and began a relationship with a beautiful woman who worked there and was twice my age and, yes, a complete opposite. I really cared for her, but the problem was that she had a twenty-one-year-old daughter, and quite honestly, I knew this would end badly; I was only twenty-four at the time. I woke up one morning and decided to leave Colorado and return to South Florida. I said goodbye to Mike and his wife and started the long trip home with less than one hundred dollars!

I once again returned to my parents' house and continued my abusive and selfish ways. Several weeks later, during a drunken stupor, I broke into a local restaurant because I was hungry, and they were closed. Who breaks into a restaurant because they have the beer munchies?

I was eventually arrested for structural burglary, and even the arresting officer was amazed that I did not touch the cash in the till, just the food in the walk-in. This was my first arrest, and I received probation even though it was a felony. My father's embarrassment must have been off the charts because I was arrested in the town where he worked for close to twenty years.

I returned to the bottled water company and slowly began saving for my own place. I met an Italian girl and once again thought I was in love. Let's call her Ann. We eventually moved into a small place together, and shortly thereafter, she told me that she was pregnant. The thoughts, pain, and guilt from Grace made me sit down and think about my life, and I knew that there was no way I was going to consider another abortion.

I remember thinking that it would be exciting to have a child and honestly hoped that this would help me mature and settle down.

I had always heard that my father was also a wild child until he got married and started a family.

Our parents were members of the same church, and that made my mother very happy. Having been married before, we were required to attend classes, and I had to receive an annulment from the church. Our parents blessed us financially, but my brother was not happy about me getting married again. He and his wife had gotten involved in a legalistic religious environment.

Ann's father cooked all the food for the reception and paid for everything. How we ever felt comfortable during the ceremony is beyond me because she was four months pregnant when we said our vows.

CHAPTER 4

The Corruptible Seed Bears Seed

It was Monday, July 18, 1983, and it appeared to be like any other day. Within a few hours, my pager went off with a 911 message, and my wife had been taken to the hospital and was in labor. Once again, His hedge of protection covered me as I drove the ten-ton route truck to the hospital like I just stole it.

When I got there, I realized that this was going to be a very long day. We had attended the Lamaze classes, and although somewhat helpful, those breathing exercises only go so far. After ten hours of sheer bliss, we were blessed with our first child, a beautiful healthy boy.

I will never forget that moment when he entered the world, the miracle of childbirth and that feeling of total joy. All of my substance abuse and tens of thousands of dollars spent on narcotics can't even compare. **"For the kingdom of God is not food and drink, but righteousness and peace and joy in the Holy Spirit" (Romans 14:17).**

We were like any young family. Money was tight, but the joy that a child brings to a young couple is another one of God's awesome blessings. I continued to be a terrible financial steward and acted like a teenager. During our first two years of our marriage, we were forced to move three times.

I began working with a grassroots investigative agency that was owned by Ann's first cousin, and she had recently announced that she was pregnant again. We were later asked to relocate further south, which was disturbing to us because both our families now lived an hour away, and so was the doctor and hospital.

The following year, we were visiting her parents for the weekend, and she went into labor late Sunday night, and my concerns of being an hour away from the hospital were taken care of by God, like everything else. **"Be anxious for nothing, but in everything by prayer and supplication, with thanksgiving, let your requests be made known to God" (Philippians 4:6).** Early Monday morning, we were blessed with a beautiful healthy baby girl. I remember thinking about how I should have been saving money the last several years instead of partying.

Several months passed, and we were blessed to move back to Palm Beach County. My father was having major health problems, and during the last ten-plus years, he had two heart attacks, a stroke, and major brain surgery. He was only in his late fifties! I remember hearing him say once to my mother, "What is the sense of living anymore?" I had a flashback to the small closet and the bug bombs and thought to myself, *You have three beautiful grandchildren to live for.* My brother had a son named Michael who was five years older than Kevin.

My brother and his wife lost their first two children back in the late seventies, and I remember thinking how could God do this to them. He was the good one who lived for God. If God would allow that to happen, what would He allow to happen to me and/or my family? Don't ever waste your time trying to figure out God's will.

I remained working as a field investigator and my wife started working nights and I watched the kids. Those lean years were rough, but the time I was able to spend with my children was priceless. I continued smoking and drinking, and by this time in my life, it was as normal as brushing my hair and teeth.

During the eighties, because of my profession and lifestyle, I had several guns drawn on me. I will not dwell on this but would like to share one story that happened. I used to occasionally visit a guy I played softball with for weed and cocaine. One evening, I called him and asked if I could stop by, which was code for "do you have any drugs?"

When I entered his neighborhood, I noticed a vehicle parked down the street and saw someone sitting in the back seat. When I was in his apartment, I told him about the vehicle and that he was probably under surveillance. We smoked some weed, and I purchased a small amount of cocaine.

When I was leaving, he noticed that my wallet had fallen out of my jeans and was on his sofa. When he threw it to me, my badge (which was not issued by the state, just a form of intimidation) fell out, and he wigged! He took out his .357 Magnum and placed the barrel to my head and insisted that I was an undercover cop. Much to my surprise, I was very calm and told him that he had better pull the trigger or put the gun away. Through God's mercy, he chose the latter. That was the last time I saw him, and his brother later told me that he moved back to Ohio.

In late 1987, I received a second felony conviction and plea bargained with the state and accepted a possession of a firearm charge instead of the three original charges that would have been mandatory prison time. My parents blessed me by bailing me out of jail and hiring an attorney to defend me. Needless to say, God showed me unbelievable mercy during the eighties.

I remember being at my parents' house on Tuesday, December 1, 1987, and had said goodbye and was sitting in my car. Suddenly, I had the strong urge to go back inside and tell my father that I loved him (that strong urge was the Holy Spirit trying to help this lost soul) but allowed Satan to convince me that I would see him on the weekend.

Three days later, my father suffered a massive heart attack and died. I remembered that strong urge that God put on my heart and how I ignored Him. No matter how good or bad your relationships are with loved ones, always tell them that you love them; it may be the last time you see them on earth. My brother and his family moved in with my mother because she was now seventy years old.

My wife and I had not been getting along for quite some time, primarily because of my behavior and our financial concerns, and had even separated for a short period of time. We had discussed divorce, but we tried to make it work because of the children. God has a plan for each of us, and if I have learned anything in my life, it is that God's ways are not our ways, and things will happen in his timing, not ours. **"Can you fathom the mysteries of God? Can you probe the limits of the Almighty" (Job 11:7)?**

In November 1988, my wife told me that she was pregnant again! Even though I was excited and have always considered children a gift from God, my financial concerns overwhelmed me. I remember thinking, *I can't afford the two I have now. How can I afford a third?* Shortly before her announcement, I had quit my job due to being overlooked for a promotion that I thought I deserved. I started doing delivery work for a 40 percent decrease in pay. *Old habits die hard.*

Prior to Ann announcing the arrival of our third child, I had agreed to bowl in the state tournament in Tampa with members of our weekly league. We were assured by her doctor that she would not have the baby for at least another two weeks, so I took Kevin, and we went to Tampa.

When we came back to the hotel on Saturday night after feasting at an AYCE buffet, I saw the phone blinking and immediately had a sick feeling in my stomach. Imagine not having a cell phone to communicate with loved ones! I called the front desk and was informed that my wife had just gone into labor and was at the hospital. Knowing that each child comes quicker and being four hours from home, I knew I would never make it but had to try. I made a bed for my son in the back seat and headed east.

His hedge of protection once again surrounded us because I was sleepy, traveling seventy miles per hour on a foggy two-lane highway during the middle of the night. **"I will never leave you or forsake you" (Joshua 1:5).** When I got to the hospital, I missed Renee's birth by an hour and had to remind myself that she was healthy, and that was all that really mattered.

During the next five months, our marriage continued to deteriorate, and due to my inability to pay our bills, we were forced to move in with her parents. They were extremely generous and blessed us by opening their home to the five of us, even though they still had children at home. I can honestly say that this period of time in my life seemed like an out-of-control tornado but was just a moderate storm.

By Thanksgiving, I decided that I could no longer live with my wife, even though we had three children under seven years old. **"It is better to dwell in the wilderness, than with a contentious and angry woman" (Proverbs 21:19).** Sometimes it gets to a point when parents are doing more harm than good staying together for the sake of the children.

We all have regrets in life, but through His grace and His wisdom, we move on. The five months that I lived with my youngest daughter, Renee, was the only time in my life that I actually lived with her. I knew that Ann's parents would provide for my children, even though I helped out financially. We only had the one vehicle, and I left it for her because of the children.

The next several months were some of the hardest in my life. I stayed with my friend Mike with whom I stayed with in Colorado years earlier. He had recently moved back to Florida. He was now divorced, and even though he did not drink, we smoked out every day.

One of the things I can be happy about at this time in my life was that every evening, I called my kids to say goodnight, which was not pleasant because I had to walk to a public phone, and my wife or her parents would answer. That Christmas morning at their house was awkward to say the least. Even to this day, when I watch the video, you can feel the tension in the room.

In February 1990, I suffered a mild heart attack because of my lifestyle and stress. My overprotective mother insisted that I stay with them, and I lived in my brother's RV which was thirty years old and not self-contained.

I started working for a very successful businessman who owned a limousine and hired me as his private driver. Although this seems exciting, it was long hours for short money but did allow me to rent a small efficiency located on Singer Island. The room was small and overpriced, but the property was located on the Lake Worth Lagoon across from Peanut Island. There was a fifty-foot dock with a cleaning station, propane grill, and patio furniture. You could catch an endless supply of snapper and be eating it fifteen minutes after you caught it.

Being the corruptible seed of Adam, I took advantage of my boss's good nature and began using the stretch at night to pick up my friends and drive them to the clubs, for a nominal fee of course, which was usually weed or cocaine. There are dozens of stories that I could tell you, but I will limit it to one.

I had driven my boss and his girlfriend to a Heart concert at the old Miami Arena and had already planned on attending because I was a big fan of Ann and Nancy. After dropping them at the door, I drove to the limo corral where I was expected to remain until they came out. I popped the trunk where I had my clothes on a hanger and to the amazement of the other drivers, changed my clothes and headed in to the concert.

I had met several ladies inside and went for a beer run and remember thinking that this facility houses thousands of people and the chance of running into my boss seemed unlikely, or so I thought. I was walking up the steps leading to my seat carrying several beers when I heard my boss say, "What do you think you are doing?" My reply was "drinking, sir."

To say he was unhappy would be an understatement. I delivered the beers and headed to the nearest exit. When I got near the exit, I heard the three ladies say "wait up." We went to the limo, smoked out, and I am sure that the other drivers are still talking about this. We lost track of time and, suddenly, the rear door opened, and my boss was standing there with a look that I could not even begin to explain. The limo was filled with smoke and, of course, the three young ladies. Why he allowed me to drive him home remains a mystery.

The following morning, I was scheduled to fly to O-Town to bowl in another state tournament because I could not ride with my friends due to the Heart concert. I overslept and made it to the ticket counter with less than ten minutes before departure. I was told that it was too late to check my bag and to take the forty pounds of bowling gear and to run as fast as I could to the gate. That was when I noticed a very attractive woman who was also late and had three suitcases. I asked if I could help and grabbed two of her bags, and we made it to the gate just as they were closing the door. We ended up sitting together, and I told her about the bowling tournament and where I was staying. She was returning from a business trip and planned on relaxing in Florida before returning up north. When we arrived, I kissed her and said goodbye. I was happy to have met her and helped out with her luggage.

When my friends picked me up, I told them what had happened, and they seemed to listen but didn't really believe me. Later that evening, when we got back to the hotel after dinner, I noticed the phone blinking. She had called and left me a voice mail. She later came by the hotel and picked me up, and we went out for drinks and had a nice evening. It was so enjoyable just talking with a sweet woman from another part of the country, and even though we were both attracted to each other, we were not intimate. We said goodbye, and I was just happy to see her again.

The next afternoon, we were at the bowling center, waiting to start the tournament when one of my friends said, "Dude, there's that girl."

When I looked up and saw her walking toward me, I was shocked and could not help but smile. I asked her why she wasn't relaxing by the pool, and she told me that she wanted to see me again. Her arrival was exciting to me, but I began wondering why this woman was here because she was way out of my league, so to speak. I began thinking about what I would do after the tournament was over because I didn't have any wheels to get home if I was going to spend time with her. Anyway, these distractions began to concern me because my head was not in the game.

Moments later, she hugged me and whispered in my ear, "Show me what you can do." Being a born show-off, I was suddenly fired up and remembered why I was there. God showed me favor that day because I bowled well enough to finish in the top twenty for the entire state, which I had never done before.

The tournament was now over, and my friends were packing up to head home. And I was down to my last twenty dollars. She asked me if I wanted to spend time with her and told me not to worry about the money. I told my friends goodbye, and they thought I was foolish for staying with someone I had just met, especially since she told me that she had a flight to return home the following morning.

We spent the night together at a high-end hotel, and the next morning, she had offered to let me use her rental car to get home. This was an incredible gesture to me because she had only known me a few days. We headed for the airport so I could drop her off. When we got in the terminal, she asked me to wait because she wanted to make a few phone calls and walked out of view. When she returned, she told me that she had rescheduled her flight for tomorrow and was going to depart from Palm Beach. We drove to my apartment and spent the afternoon swimming in the lagoon, walking on the beach, grilling fresh fish, and stayed up most of the night talking and...

The next day, we went to the airport, and that was the last time I ever saw or spoke with her. I thought about not sharing the following thoughts but feel as though it is important. Remember I was at the Heart concert the evening before I met her? Well, they had a very popular song at the time called "All I Want to Do" which is about a married woman who seeks a man to get her pregnant. We must have heard this song a few dozen times while we were together. Coincidence?

I continued playing chauffeur, and within a few weeks, I had stayed out all night with my buddies, met a young lady at a club and went back to her house, and I did not wake up until the early afternoon. I never picked up my boss for work and, later that day, dropped off the limo and was terminated. I ended up having to move out of the rental and back to the RV.

On Thanksgiving morning, I picked up the kids so they could spend the holiday with my mother and our family. I remembered that it had been exactly one year since I bailed on my wife. Later that day, I was dropping off the kids and ran into my prior boss from the investigative agency who asked me to return to work and run one of his branch offices.

I agreed, and after hiring a new staff for the Fort Lauderdale office, he transferred me to O-Town so I could do the same. I worked long hours for short money but was happy to be doing something that I enjoyed. I was staying with my sister-in-law (who was the office manager) and her boyfriend and had to sleep on their couch because I could not afford an apartment because of my wages and the money I was giving to my wife for child support.

I began to miss my children dearly, so every Friday when I got out of work, I drove the three hours back to South Florida and spent the weekends with them. My mother and brother were a blessing to all of us because I had very limited funds to entertain the children. Thank God my parents had put in a swimming pool after I moved out. I would drop them off late Sunday afternoon and return to O-Town and work my seventy- to eighty-hour schedule and then do it again every Friday.

In July 1991, I had saved enough money to finally get an apartment and asked my wife (yes, we were still legally married) if Kevin and Kristy could spend the summer with me because the weekend commute was killing me. Much to my surprise, she said yes, and they ended up living with me for ten years. I had asked for all three, but Renee was only two years old. I remember how tight money was after paying my fixed weekly expenses. I had less than a hundred dollars a week for food, entertainment, gasoline, school aftercare, etc., etc.

Looking back, the less money I had the happier I was. **"No one can serve two masters; for he either will hate the one or love the other, or else he will be loyal to the one and despise the other. You cannot serve God and mammon" (Matthew 6:24).**

I continued to smoke and drink but reduced my consumption greatly. When I watch the video from those days and see my kids riding their bikes and being kids, I always cry.

Looking back, my biggest regret during this time was that I did not raise my children in a Christian household with biblical truths, but you can't teach something you don't know or want to know. **"Train up a child in the way he should go, and when he is old he will not depart from it" (Proverbs 22:6).**

My brother had been diagnosed with leukemia and died on February 20, 1992. He was thirty-seven. My brother and I were never really close, but I did love him. He was my only brother. I remember thinking about his life, and once again, how could God allow this to happen? He now had a thirteen-year-old son, a wife, and Mother who depended on him, and he was in the prime of his life.

He had already taken his first two children, and quite honestly, I became very confused about a God that would allow this to happen. I am not saying this was God's plan, but I would have never returned home, met my current wife, and my additional two children would never have been born if he was not called home.

I transferred back to South Florida because I wanted to take care of my mother. I was a complete ass to my brother's wife and son and would publicly like to ask for their forgiveness. I had basically told them that I was moving back into the house to take care of my mother, and that they would have to move out and find another place to live. Is that how you treat someone who had taken care of your mother for five years? Forgive me, Cheryl and Michael.

Since my children came to live with me, I had only been on a few dates and had two weeks paid vacation coming. Kevin and Kristy stayed with their mother, and I asked a family friend to stay with my mom and flew to San Diego to see my gal pal. It was my thirty-fifth birthday.

She picked me up from the airport in a stretch limo with a chilled Magnum of Jordan and a few joints. She had stocked her kitchen with prime meats, fresh fish and shellfish, some vintage wine, and the area where she lived was very close to the beach.

A few days later, we drove down to Mexico and spent the entire day at a bar and restaurant that was built on the side of a cliff. I had decided to make a movie out of my vacation and began filming from the time I drove to Fort Lauderdale until I returned. I shot about eight hours of tape, and I think it turned out very well.

I spent ten days in Cali, and the time there was relaxing and just what I needed. Although I enjoyed spending time with her, I considered her a friend with benefits and knew that it would never be anything more.

While in Southern California, I was fortunate enough to visit my friend Tommy who had been in the car accident two decades earlier. We had a nice lunch and he showed me the studio where he worked and I tried not to be starstruck when we visited where several well-known sitcoms were filmed. Although I enjoyed spending time with him, I could not help but think how living in LA had changed him.

When I left San Diego, my gal pal and I made plans for her to visit me in South Florida in a few months. I never even considered that I was still legally married and was committing adultery by spending time with her. Ann was now living with one of our old neighbors, and they were raising Renee. Coincidence?.

CHAPTER 5 ────

The Corruptible Seed
Finds His Abigail

After returning home, I went to go see a friend of mine from work who bowled on the company team because she told me that she wanted me to meet one of the girls she bowled with. I brought my three children, and try to picture what I must have looked like. I was carrying Renee, Kristy was holding onto my legs, and Kevin was holding my hand. She later told me that when she first looked at me, she thought, *Look at that poor guy with all those kids.*

I started talking with my coworker for a few minutes, and then I saw her. She was a bright light in my darkened world. She had a long loose perm, big red glasses, and her name means a pure heart, yes, my beloved Kathleen. If you looked up Plain Jane in the dictionary, it would have her picture. I have never believed in love at first sight, just lust at first sight, but she was different.

I was attracted to her immediately, but she wanted nothing to do with me because of a recent break up. I gave her my number and hoped for the best. Several weeks later, she finally called, and we had dinner at my favorite Italian restaurant which also turned out to be her favorite. If I had not suggested this restaurant, she might not have ever agreed to meet me. Thank You, Jesus.

We continued seeing each other, and she was different from any other woman that I had ever met and, of course, a complete opposite. She was extremely honest, caring, and had a serious relationship with

Jesus Christ. She was a good friend, an excellent stepmother, and generally cared about my mother who was now seventy-five.

I had forgotten about my gal pal from San Diego, and in late July, she called me to let me know that she was in town and when should she come by. Try to explain that to someone who you just started dating. For one of the few times in my life I tried to do the right thing and had her stay at my house, and we stayed with Kathleen (a.k.a. Kathy, Katie, and Isaiah).

A few days later, we had a birthday party for my oldest daughter, Kristy, at a skating facility, and Ann, Katie, and my gal pal were all there. Can you say awkward? It reminded me of the same event that happened close to two decades earlier. My gal pal returned to Cali, and Katie was not shy about telling her to hit the bricks.

Katie had never been married, and I was as honest as I could be with her about my past without sending her running for the hills. I do recall telling her that I was divorced because I knew she would never date a legally married man. Within a few months, she moved out of her apartment and moved in with us.

It was Christmas Eve, and we never went to bed and stayed up wrapping presents. That was one of the best Christmas mornings ever. Later in the day, we visited Ann and her boyfriend so Renee could open her presents. God's grace was shown through Ann because there was no longer any animosity between us, and both of us were happy with our new partners.

Katie and I had planned a trip to Michigan for later that day so Katie could visit her family during the holidays. We left at midnight, and my goal was to make it to Tennessee and stay over. After fourteen hours of driving, we arrived outside of Gatlinburg and got a room for the night.

Considering that I had been up for close to two days, getting some rest should have been my priority. I had visited the ski resort before and wanted the kids to see it because they had never seen snow. Katie tried to reason with me, but being a stubborn Italian Taurus, I insisted we will be back in a few hours.

Being clueless that this area has something called the festival of lights parade during the Christmas holidays, the traffic made the

101 in LA look like the country. What should have taken less than an hour took us close to four.

When we reached the ski resort, it was dark, cold, and closing. The looks I received were getting worse by the minute because we had basically been in a small compact since midnight. As I began driving down the mountain, I realized that we were losing our brakes, and I was using the gears and emergency brake to try and slow down. Katie was yelling at me, "Why are you driving so fast?" I was gaining speed and started thinking, *How am I going to stop this vehicle?*

I finally told Katie what was going on, and we asked God to help us because the gears and emergency brake were not working. Within one hundred yards after praying, our brakes were restored after pumping the lines. **"Ask, and it will be given to you; seek, and you will find; knock, and it will be opened to you"** (Matthew **7:7).**

We got back to the hotel and enjoyed a good night of slumber. When I woke up and looked outside, it had snowed all night, and that fresh blanket of powder looked like a Thomas Kincade painting. Kevin and Kristy played in the snow for an hour, and I truly believe that God blessed my children with that snow because the weather forecast did not call for snow until after the New Year.

Later that day, we arrived at her parents' house and received a warm and loving welcome, even though her father did not seem to approve of me having children from a prior marriage. Years later, I was told that her father told her not to get involved with me because I had too much baggage; he may have been right. Her father was much like me, a smoker and drinker, and over time, we became very close.

I met her four sisters and three brothers and their spouses and realized why she was so nice. She had been raised with strong Christian beliefs and values. She showed me where she grew up, where she went to high school, and where she used to work. I truly love her family, but meeting the potential in-laws and extended family can be stressful and exhausting.

We stayed till after New Year's and then headed south with brakes and His continued hedge of protection. The long drive home allowed me to tell her that I was still legally married, which had been bothering me for several months. She was not happy but understood why I lied. Within a few months, Ann and I filed the necessary paperwork to dissolve the marriage.

During the next several months, we spent the majority of our free time together, and I had never felt so close to anyone before. She was an unbelievable girlfriend and had a natural desire to be a mother and was such a blessing to my children. I never had any sisters and did not know much about raising young girls. Thank you, honey.

May 29, 1993, was our one-year anniversary, and I had planned on proposing. We spent the weekend in the romantic city of Saint Augustine and went window-shopping and antiquing which gives her great joy. Later that evening, we went to an expensive restaurant, and when the moment seemed right, I got down on my right knee and popped the question. She looked at me without any real emotion and said, "I have to think about it. Can I let you know later?" How do you respond to that? We still had a nice evening, and the following afternoon, she said yes.

We set the date for later that year and planned on having the wedding in Michigan. Her parents and siblings blessed us beyond measure financially and by also planning the entire event. When her parents found out that I had been married twice before, it was quite a shock to them why their daughter would want to get involved with someone like me.

The day before our scheduled wedding, we were trying to get to the airport, which seemed like the scene from *Home Alone*. It was late November. Anyway, the boarding gate was packed, and as they started boarding, the attendant called my name and asked me if the five of us would take a later flight in exchange for five free airline vouchers. Getting bumped with three kids and a three-hour delay was not worth the aggravation, and besides, we would miss the wedding rehearsal and dinner. We boarded our scheduled flight and lost the free vouchers. At least we didn't get dragged off a plane.

The wedding was simple, and it was a joy meeting her extended family and friends. The reception was crazy fun, and we spent our first night as husband and wife in a very nice hotel, even though it was freezing outside.

A few months after returning home, I was at work, and the receptionist told me that I had a visitor who identified himself as a DCF investigator. He told me that he was there because someone had filed a formal complaint with his office alleging parental abuse! He wanted to know why we were leaving my mother alone every day. I knew that she was not herself anymore, but I guess I was being naive about what was going on at the house while we were gone.

After numerous doctor visits, we were told that she was in the advanced stages of Alzheimer's and needed twenty-four-hour supervision by a trained professional, and we were forced to put her into an assisted living facility. Out of the hundreds of regrets in my life, that is one that is at the top of the list. My mother devoted her entire life to her family, and suddenly, I was too busy to care. I love you, Mom. Please forgive me.

In July of '94, I was offered the opportunity to purchase the branch office that I had been managing, and my only thought was about the amount of money I could make. Greed is a very powerful weapon used by Satan. I did not consider my children, my wife, nor asked God what He thought. I borrowed the initial investment from Tommy and began working fourteen- to sixteen-hour days, and although I had tripled our income, what was the cost?

Katie and I had been discussing having children, even though I had mixed feelings about having another child in my late thirties. Our life together was fruitful, and we truly loved spending time alone without the kids. I think that spending time together without the children is essential to a long and loving marriage.

During the end of April 1995, we went to Don Shula's Hotel in Miami Lakes for the weekend to celebrate Katie's birthday. It was one of the few trips that we did not plan a full day of activities. We just spent time together and relaxed. **"Be still and know that I am God" (Psalm 46:10).**

Several months later, I had returned from a business trip from Tallahassee because another company office had become available. When I was dropped off at the house, she was glowing, and I knew what she was going to say. What I didn't know was that she was pregnant with twins! What! I will have five children (six—sorry, Grace), and I will be in my late fifties when they graduate high school? Our selfish and corruptible nature always consider ourselves and our needs first? It suddenly dawned on me that I will be the same age that my mother was when I was growing up. God has a sense of humor!

My wife told me point-blank, "Do not buy another office. You are spreading yourself too thin."

Over the years, I have given her the nickname Isaiah because she is usually right about anything that deals with people and/or the future. Well, being stubborn and selfish, I purchased another office anyway and usually sat quietly whenever I heard "I told you."

A major concern for us was where we were going to live with the addition to our family. Our current home was comfortable but under a thousand square feet and only had one bathroom. We spent the next several months looking at larger homes in our area and also property in North Florida. Anytime you have an emotional attachment to an asset, your thinking and reasoning is altered.

We decided that we would do a major renovation on our current home and double the square footage and do some much needed upgrades. I should have listened to a trusted friend who suggested we doze it and start from scratch. We put our thoughts and ideas on hold and concentrated on getting ready for the babies.

Although we frequently attended church as a family, it was out of obligation and not to praise and worship our Creator. We returned to the Catholic Church, and I usually sat there and thought about work or what football games were on later in the day. I did not really listen to what they were saying and, quite honestly, have always had a problem with organized religion and their monthly budgets.

Katie was three weeks away from her due date and looked like she was ready to pop. Her parents came to Florida to help us prepare for the new arrivals. Their presence was much needed but also a strain on the family, mostly because of our small living conditions. Between the pressures at work, raising the children, and the problems at home, my stress level was off the charts. **"Come to me, all you**

who labor and are heavy laden, and I will give you rest" (Matthew 11:28).

The following statement will reveal my true character at this time in my life. Even though I continued working long hours, I would remain at the office drinking and smoking weed after hours because I just did not want to deal with the pressures and problems at home.

My wife's parents are very loving and helpful people, and having eight children, they have very strong parental instincts and routines. They were telling me when to eat, what to eat, when to go to bed and had taken over my house. I should have just been grateful for their blessings, but I am used to having my own way.

On February 7, we visited the doctor. It was the day before her due date. Within a few minutes, I knew something was wrong because of the way they were whispering. He finally told us that we needed to get checked into the hospital at once because one of the babies may be in distress. Anyone who works in a hospital should have a special saint status because even though you are freaking out, it is just another day at work for them. They comforted Katie, and after a few hours, they assured us that both babies were fine.

That morning, I had woken up with an unbearable toothache, and it continued to get worse as the day progressed. I was assured that the delivery would not be until the following morning. Haven't I heard this before? There was no way that I was going to miss another delivery. My mother-in-law and Katie's sister Judy said to go to the dentist, and they would stay with her.

I ended up having a root canal, and Dr. Pain Maker was kind enough to give me a dozen pain pills which, of course, I took over the next few hours. The following morning, they wheeled her into the delivery room and started prepping her for a C-section. Her girl-friend Kristen had done the birthing classes with Katie because of my brutal schedule, and the three of us were in the OR. That was a moment I will never forget.

Back at the house, it was very confining, to say the least. We had both babies in our ten-feet-by-eleven-feet room along with the changing table, crib, dresser, hundreds of infant clothes, and the kitchen was now a bottle factory. Anyone who has ever had multiples understands that there is always something to do. Her parents stayed another *month*, and after an emotional outbreak on my part, they decided to return to Michigan. My older children were heaven-sent because they helped us every day as I continued working long hours and was seldom around to help out.

A few months later, we had the twins baptized, and some of Katie's siblings and her parents came into town. The first day was very uncomfortable, to say the least, because it was the first time I had seen her parents since they left, and everyone knew about my abusive behavior. I tried to make the best of the situation. and the baptism was a very special moment.

I have mixed feelings regarding infant baptism, but if it brings others joy, what's the harm? I was taught to believe that a child who dies young goes to heaven because of their sinless nature, but there's that original sin again. I think that we are hopeful regarding a child's death, even though I have not read any scriptures that clearly define this. Were we led to believe that God helps those who help themselves? Haven't seen that one either. Bottom line, it comes down to our level of faith.

A few months later, we found a contractor to do the renovation, and anyone who has ever lived in a property while it is being renovated knows the hell they put you through. There is always a problem dealing with people who treat your home like a jobsite, even though it is. We soon realized that this dust-filled environment was no place for two small children, and my wife took the babies to Michigan and spent time with her family.

Due to the house being close to uninhabitable, I was spending the majority of my time at the Tallahassee office, which I had moved into a three-bedroom town house. The children were out of school for the summer and staying with their mother. I decided to drive to Michigan to see my family.

While I was in Michigan, I began to notice that my wife was suddenly too busy to have a relationship with her husband because of the never-ending work with the twins. I tried to lighten her load and help out, but when someone has a routine, it is easier to do more damage than good. My wife decided to stay with her family in Michigan for another few months.

The renovation was finally completed near the end of the year, and we were all together again as a family. We had designed a twenty-two-feet-by-twelve-feet room for the twins and a very large master bedroom and bath for us. It was such a pleasure finally having the space we needed, but the renovation had doubled our mortgage. I was making the most money I had ever earned, but it was being spent as quickly as I was earning it.

The next several months were starting to get to me because of the pressures at work, and once again, Isaiah was right; I never should have bought the second office. I had now moved the office from Tallahassee to Pensacola, which was another two hundred miles west and spent a great deal of time commuting the six hundred miles and staying there for days at a time. I ended up moving the office into a two-bedroom apartment because it was cheaper than the money I was spending on hotels. Without allowing God to guide me, the time away from my wife and kids started a separation between us that only God could fix.

It was June 2, 1997, and I was working in the Pensacola area and having breakfast at a Waffle House while interviewing potential new hires. My pager went off (cell service was still limited in this area), and it was my wife. When I called her back, she said, "Your mother died this morning!" No warning, no "I have some bad news," just the woman you have known for forty years has died. My wife is not the type of person who sugarcoats things. She is very blunt. I find it funny that things that originally attract us to woman, we later hold against them.

Although I felt obligated to take care of the hundreds of details for my mom, this just added to my stress. I did deliver the eulogy for her in her favorite church and was later told by her friends and the family members that still remained that it was special. Several weeks later, it occurred to me that I had lost my father, my brother, and my mom in five-year increments and started wondering about 2002.

CHAPTER 6

The Corruptible Seed in a Sin-Filled Valley

It was now the summer of 1998, and I had continued my brutal work schedule and grew further and further from my family. Thinking that money and possessions bring joy, I purchased a very expensive RV, and even though we had several great trips and vacations, I should have been saving money for my children and helping those less fortunate. We had decided to take a trip to Michigan in the RV and visit her parents and family. This was our maiden voyage, and the seven of us had a great time for a few days.

After only one day in Michigan, Katie and I had a terrible fight because she was stressed out because of the twins and also because of my attitude and selfishness. I was about to make another colossal mistake. Not wanting to deal with her and her family, I told the older kids to get their things together, packed up the RV, and we left my wife and twins in Michigan. Who does that? Someone who runs from responsibility and is selfish and self-centered.

The four of us went camping in the mountains of West Virginia at Twin Falls State Park. Almost every trip or vacation in this RV seemed to be an adventure. When we were approaching the state park, I misread the sign and started driving on what we would soon discover to be the hiking trail and not the entrance to the campsite.

This was not a pop-up camper; it was a twelve-foot-high thirty-three-foot-long C class! I remember commenting how rustic the state park and campsites must be. Within a few minutes, the road had turned into a small trail which was much lower than our roof and only wide enough for a small compact. I had gone too far to try and back up and had to relandscape the hiking trail as we continued driving.

When I finally reached a clearing approximately three to four miles later, there were a few homes and the gentleman (and I use that term loosely), whose property I turned around on, was now standing there with a twelve gauge thinking, *How the hell did you get that RV up here?* We were able to return down the hiking trail and finally got settled for the night. We spent several days in West Virginia and then visited Jacksonville and Daytona Beach for a few days before returning home.

My wife and twins stayed in Michigan for several weeks, and quite honestly, I did not expect them to return. At this point in time, most of her family strongly disliked me, and I am sure that they were telling her not to return to Florida. She decided to fly into Greenville, South Carolina, with her sister Judy who is a flight attendant. I drove the RV and went and picked up my family.

It was very nice seeing them again, but I soon realized that we were now living separate lives and were only married because the state said we were. She had the twins and someone to fund her life, and I had my career and abusive lifestyle. After a few weeks, we decided that a separation was best, and she remained in the house with all of the children. I lived in an RV park, and my substance abuse increased.

I can't tell you how many times in my life I drove home drunk without any memory of getting there. That is very alarming, to say the least, when the last thing you remember is standing in some bar twenty miles from your house, and then you wake up in bed the next morning. Consider that if you don't believe we have guardian angels that God sends to protect us, sometimes from ourselves.

I hired a manager for the Pensacola office and concentrated on the local office because our sales were down 20 percent because of my summer vacations. Being an alcoholic and thinking that I had not done anything wrong, I began to have an emotional and flirting affair with a younger woman that I had hired for the local office. This went on for several months, and even though I never slept with her, I was still being unfaithful to my wife.

I finally came to my senses and returned to the house just before Christmas and no longer thought that the grass might be greener elsewhere. I really tried to be a better father and husband, but the stress of the job and abusive behavior to my mind and body began to take its toll, again.

By March of 1999, I was completely burned out at work and ready for a nervous breakdown. Working one-hundred-plus hours per week for close to five years had finally caught up with me. I worked out a buyout for the two offices with my boss which turned out to be a nightmare. At this point in time, I just wanted out regardless of monies lost.

We ended up in litigation, and it cost us everything we had for never-ending legal expenses. Most of our investments, life insurance policies, the Jet Ski, and our savings account were all liquidated, but the peace and joy that I now had from not working my schedule was worth every penny. I finally began to listen, learn, and love my family again. I was able to spend some quality time with them, but not working soon became a concern.

We settled with my ex-partner and agreed to a multi-year settlement extending over the next few years. I agreed to not work as an investigator in the state of Florida for a short period of time. I began to once again realize that money is not the path to happiness. We had basically lost over two hundred thousand in the litigation and settlement.

Later that summer, we decided that the four of us would take a vacation to Michigan in the RV. We spent a week in Michigan visiting her parents and her extended family. I had not seen her family since the prior summer when I abandoned them in Michigan. I did my best to apologize, but some are better than others at forgiveness. It was a very special time for us as a family as I tried rebuilding our relationship.

We were traveling in Southeast Ohio, and I saw a sign for Salt Fork State Park which also had a championship golf course. We stopped at the pro shop, and when I saw the course, I was excited. It had hills and valleys and was not like any course that I had ever seen. We made it to the campsite, and I decided I would play a round of golf.

Much to my surprise, the course did not provide transportation from the campsites to the links. I asked them how far it was from the campgrounds, and they said ten to eleven miles. They also told me that there was a hiking trail to the golf course which was only five to six miles.

I left the campgrounds at about twelve and figured I would be at the links by about two and told my wife I should be back about dusk. An hour into the hiking trail, I realized that this was not Florida, and I could not walk the three to four miles an hour I was accustomed to. This hiking trail had extreme hills and ridges, and all I could think about was why I didn't leave my clubs at the pro shop when I was there.

I was still about two miles from the links and wanted to share this and hope you can appreciate the humor. As I continued walking, I could hear people laughing, and when I approached a clearing near the lake, I saw four teenagers sitting in a boat on the shore drinking and carrying on.

I took out my seven iron, and when they saw me, they became confused why someone was hiking with golf clubs. I approached the boat and asked them if they had seen a titlist? They just looked at me and said no. I told them what was going on and asked them if they wanted to smoke. One of them asked me if I was Jesus. We ended up smoking a few joints, and they gave me a ride in the boat and dropped me off a half mile from the links.

Anyway, when I arrived, the employees and golfers at the pro shop looked at me like I was crazy, which I was. When I told them I walked from the campground, they were so impressed that they let me play for free and gave me a six pack of beer on ice and two hot dogs. The older woman working at the pro shop told me that she would drive me back to the campsite when I finished. I played one of the best rounds I had ever played, and I only mentioned this story because of what happened after I finished playing. It is the difference between reality and perception.

When I returned to the pro shop, the older woman that I had spoken with had gone home for the day. A beautiful eighteen- to nineteen-year-old was the only one left, and she asked me if I was the guy who needed a ride back to the campgrounds. She told me that she still had about an hour till she got off and would drive me then and continued feeding me beers for free.

When we got to the campgrounds, I asked her to drop me off at the entrance, and I would walk the rest of the way, but she said it is not a problem. Well, it was a big problem for me. Keeping in mind my past track record, I could only imagine what my wife would think getting dropped off by a beautiful young woman, intoxicated, and three hours late.

When we got to the RV, my wife and kids were standing outside, and when she saw this young lady with me, well, you get the picture. Even though I had not done anything wrong, it continued to water the seed of doubt with my wife. The rest of that evening was not very pleasant.

The following morning, I convinced Katie to let me play another round of golf when we broke camp, and she and the twins could come with me. She was not thrilled about spending a few hours in the hot August sun, but she knew that the kids would enjoy it. The video and photos I took of the kids are still some of my favorites.

Having been married in a nondenominational church, Katie began hinting that she would like to renew our wedding vows in our church. I was trying to get closer to the Lord but, once again, was trying through my flesh and not my heart and spirit. I agreed to renew our vows, and it was a very exciting time in our lives because we were trying to start over as a family.

What started out as a simple wedding ceremony with only our closest friends and family turned into a ten-thousand-dollar event! It all started when I asked my wife what she was going to wear, and her answer was "my wedding dress, of course." It seemed reasonable, but that would mean I would need to wear a tux, and from there, everything just snowballed. Kevin would be my best man, Johnny would be a ring bearer, and my father-in-law would be insulted if he was not part of the wedding party. Kristy and Renee would stand up with my wife, and Megan would be the flower girl.

Now we were renting four tuxes, buying three new dresses with shoes and, of course, visiting a salon before the big day. We would also need flowers, a photographer, someone to take video, a limo, invitations, and a wedding reception. We invited about forty people, and my father-in-law thought I was crazy when I invited my ex-boss because I was trying to extend the olive branch.

We went to Maggie Valley, North Carolina, for a honeymoon because we never really had one back in '93. I played golf most every day, and my wife just relaxed and enjoyed a few days away from motherhood. The highlight of the trip was when we attended church at a small little building in a beautiful one-hundred-year-old wood-and- stone A-frame building named Saint Margaret's Catholic Church. The area behind the altar had stained-glass windows which highlighted the Smokey Mountains which was absolutely beautiful. If you are ever looking for a small beautiful church in the mountains for a wedding, give them a call.

Shortly after returning home, I received a certified letter from the IRS stating that I owed ten thousand dollars for back taxes, which was absolutely true. Well, the thoughts and plans of opening a small business had ended before they even began.

Being unable to work in Florida as an investigator, we discussed moving to Michigan so we could have a fresh start and also so the twins could live near their extended family. I sent out several resumes to agencies in Michigan and had positive feedback. I told them that I would contact them when we were in the area.

In April of 2001, we decided to take a trip to Michigan to see her family and to also interview for a job as an investigator. The twins were now five and had never been to Disney World, so we spent a full day at the Magic Kingdom and also visited Old Town in nearby Kissimmee. When we were window-shopping in Old Town, my wife was looking at a beautiful pair of diamond-and-ruby earrings which cost much more than I wanted to spend, but my wife's fortieth birthday was in a few days. As we continued window-shopping, I told my wife I had to use the restroom and returned to the shop and bought the earrings.

When we got to Michigan, her family had made arrangements for a birthday party at a restaurant for the big forty. My wife seemed irritated when I gave her the earrings and asked me why I would buy them. I will never understand how a woman's mind works.

Having failed with the earrings, I needed to do something else for her birthday. I planned a weekend to Cleveland, Ohio, for us and her sister Judy to attend a Joyce Meyer conference because they had seen Joyce before and really enjoyed her message. I had heard of her and listened to a few of her teachings but was just trying to do something nice for my wife.

The three of us drove to Cleveland and I truly enjoyed her message, and at one point, I began to feel the presence of God and His thickness. I suddenly smelt something that I can only describe as a mixture of fresh flowers and baked bread. **"Now thanks be to God who always leads us to triumph in Christ, and through us diffuses the fragrance of His knowledge in every place. For we are to God the fragrance of Christ among those who are being saved and among those who are perishing" (2 Corinthians 2:14–15).** I think that was the first time that I could feel His presence and began to wonder about God and my salvation.

On the drive back to Michigan, Judy blessed me with her knowledge of Christ and the Bible and had planted a seed that would still take a decade to germinate because of my selfishness and disobedience. We left Michigan a few days later after I had secured employment with a local agency, and we had decided to move back once we could make the proper arrangements.

We had numerous repairs to make on the older section of the house if we wanted to rent it out. We were able to spend quite a bit of time with Kevin, Kristy, and Renee, and I could not help but feel that they were not happy that we were moving out of state with the twins. They were eighteen, sixteen, and twelve. Deep down, my concerns were that this might cause a further separation between us, but I knew it was time to listen to my wife and start living for ourselves.

We rented out our house, rented the largest truck we could find, and tried to get both vehicles to Michigan. This trip was going to be an adventure and was not planned very well because we only had a few weeks to get everything done. We did not have much money, and we had not found a place to live, but it seemed exciting to start over again.

The twins had just turned five, and that is one of my favorite ages for children. The actual trip was extremely stressful, and allow me to explain why. The four of us were traveling in the small cab of the moving truck and towing our vehicle. I never even considered that the children were not in car seats and/or seat belts, and those of you with children understand how restless they become after a short period of time. Their innocent questions, comments, and views are one of God's blessings when we find ourselves stressed out.

Three days later, we arrived in Michigan with thirty eight dollars, and we ended up living in her sister's basement for three months, and all of us sleeping in one bed. The Lord certainly has a way of humbling us, if we don't do it on our own.

I was now making a fraction of my prior salary, but starting over in a state that I had never lived in was exciting. I once again was concerned about money and how would we ever be able to save enough to get our own place. **"Why are you fearful? O you of little faith" (Matthew 8:26).**

After a few months, my wife was hired by a major retailer and the twins were now in preschool and we enjoyed being around her family and having a much simpler lifestyle. We started attending a grace-filled church on a regular basis, and I even attended a Saturday morning bible study with my wife and her sisters when I was not working, mostly at the request of Judy.

I was beginning to get it, and God was trying to work through me, even though I continued smoking and drinking. I really did try, but I was trying to achieve something through my own ability and my flesh, and we should all know by now how that turns out. I tried to understand what the leader of the Bible study was talking about, but this was an advanced study with people that had been walking with the Lord for years. **"The first of the first fruits of your land**

you shall bring into the house of the Lord your God. You shall not boil a young goat in its mother's milk" (Exodus 23:19). That last sentence means don't overwhelm new believers with the Word.

In 1999, I had sold our last asset, a commercial office space, and did owner financing and held the paper. In September of 2001, I received a call from the buyer's wife who informed me that her husband had just died from cancer, and she wanted to pay off all debt and scheduled a closing for later that month.

I flew back to South Florida for the closing, and our equity was a few thousand dollars which gave us the money to move into a rental. Jehovah Jireh (provider) always has a plan. This also gave me the opportunity to drive our second vehicle back to Michigan.

Like most people, I will never forget where I was on Tuesday, September 11, 2001. I had just walked out of my employer's office in Livonia, Michigan, and the DJ on the radio thought it was a joke. Within a few minutes, everyone on the highway turned their lights on and began beeping their horns. The rental we had found was near an air force base, and I remember wondering if another attack was coming.

Later that week, I was working in Dearborn, Michigan, which has the largest Islamic population in the country. The tension was red lined, and I could not help but feel anger toward these people, even though they had not done anything to me or our country.

On Halloween day, my wife was with the kids, and I decided to play a round of golf, which seemed harmless enough. I started drinking beer and smoking early, and that is usually the start of something bad. And today was no exception.

After I finished golfing, I went to the lounge and started drinking Grand Mariner and saw an attractive woman sitting at the bar talking with her three friends. When I heard them making dinner plans, I asked if I could join them. Once again, I allowed my corruptible seed to convince myself that I was not doing anything wrong; it was just dinner.

Years later, I heard one of my favorite pastors at a Moody Men's conference say something that explains why we allow ourselves to behave the way we do. His statement was "A thought becomes an action. Actions define our character. Our character develops our habits, and our habits determine our destiny." Thank you for that Alistair Begg. An incredible book titled *Battlefield of the Mind* by Joyce Meyer explains this in greater detail.

We went to an expensive restaurant, and trying to be a big shot, I picked up the tab which was over three hundred dollars. I continued drinking throughout the evening and later found myself being intimate with one of the ladies in the parking area of the restaurant. I woke up the next morning at home with no memory of driving there, and once again, thank You for Your hedge of protection and guardian angels.

Several days later, I decided to return to the golf course to apologize to the young lady who worked there and try to explain that I had too much to drink that evening. As soon as she saw me, she smiled and said, "I was hoping that I would see you again."

That comment would prove to be one of the crossroads in my life and also in my character, or the lack thereof. A loving husband, father, and child of Christ would have remembered why he came there. She asked if I was available for dinner because she wanted to pay me back for treating her and her friends to such an expensive dinner. **"No temptation has overtaken you except such as is common to man; but God is faithful, who will not allow you to be tempted beyond what you are able, but with the temptation will also make the way of escape, that you may be able to bear it" (1 Corinthians 10:13).** I accepted and called my wife and told her I got called into work. Without Christ in your life, the expression once a cheater, always a cheater is usually accurate.

After having dinner with her and several bottles of wine later, we went back to her house, and I spent the night. I had once again made a bad situation worse. Not only had I committed adultery on my wife, again, but I had also told this woman that I was not married. Our affair continued for several weeks, and I found myself continuing to lie to both her and my wife because of pleasures of the flesh.

I stopped going to church and Bible study because I felt too much like a hypocrite. During the second week of December, I did the unthinkable; I sat down with Katie and told her what was going on. Isaiah told me that she figured as much and asked what did I want to do. I told her that I wanted to move out and live with my girlfriend. Who does that to their family two weeks before Christmas?

Even though my wife was hurt, she knew me better than I knew myself, and she later told me that it was a pleasure not having me around. She also told me that right after Christmas, God told her in a dream to forgive me because I did not know what I was doing. I forwarded our weekly settlement checks for her and the kids. If her parents and siblings had disliked me before, they were now furious, and I am sure she heard it from her father.

I continued living my abusive, drunken, and selfish lifestyle, and when my older kids had heard what was going on, they wanted nothing to do with me. After New Year's, my girlfriend told me that she usually vacationed in Florida until March or April. We drove to Marco Island and spent the next several weeks drinking, smoking, and playing golf every day. Sadly, I chose the evils of this world and pleasures of the flesh over my own family.

Weeks later, my wife called to tell me that she was planning a birthday party for the twins and thought it would be a good idea if I attended because the twins were upset that I was no longer around. I booked a flight back to Michigan so I could try to celebrate their sixth birthday.

Katie had planned a party at a local bowling center where my brother-in law Don worked part time. Even though I enjoyed seeing my kids, my brother-in-law and I came close to exchanging blows.

Several days after the party, I was driving my kids to school and had a flight to return to Florida later that day. Through the innocence of a child and His wisdom, my plans were about to change. My son looked at me with his big blue eyes and said, "Why don't you love me anymore?" That comment broke my heart, and through divine intervention, I realized how selfish and foolish I had been.

I never flew back to Florida, and Kathleen allowed me to move back in. And I vowed on that day that I would try to be a better husband and father, again. My wife was called foolish, stupid, and every other name you can think of for allowing me back into her life. As I said before, she took her wedding vows very seriously, even though she had biblical grounds for a divorce.

I began to realize that the lives of my children were more important than my own selfish agenda and they needed a strong father and my wife needed emotional and financial security. We remained in Michigan for several months, until my wife told me that she really didn't like living there because of the brutal winters.

Now that our house was available again, we decided to move back to Florida, and I interviewed with a company based out of O-Town. I began working with them the following week and the older kids seemed happy that we were back in South Florida.

A few weeks before Christmas, my boss called and told me that they had just secured a huge client based out of New York and had been given two dozen surveillances. He asked if I was available to work in New York for the next several weeks. Even though I was not thrilled about working in the frozen tundra, his sales pitch was that I could work as many hours as I wanted, regardless of overtime.

I agreed, and two of us were flown to New York and received large SUVs for transportation. The second investigator had family in Brooklyn, which was a plus because I was able to have my own hotel room. The cases I received were located in Queens, Brooklyn, Long Island, and the Bronx.

Everything was fine for about a week, and I was billing 12–14 hours a day. One evening, I visited an Outback restaurant for dinner, and when I tried to settle up with the company credit card, it was denied. I called the office and received a message stating that the phone had been temporary disconnected, and my boss refused to answer his cell phone. I returned to the hotel, packed up my gear, and drove back to Florida with the rental and with very limited funds. I was able to get paid only because of the video evidence that I had in my possession.

CHAPTER 7

The Corruptible Seed in a Storm

Since I was no longer under contractual obligations regarding the mediation settlement, I opened another agency and tried to learn from my prior mistakes and shortcomings. My wife continued working full time, and the twins were starting school. I ran the business out of our house and had hired a few investigators.

Within a year, we were doing very well, and I had begun to rebuild my relationships and trust with my family, even though my relationship with the older kids was still lacking any real depth. Kevin returned home after living with his mother while we were in Michigan. He was now nineteen.

We attended a local church on a regular basis, mostly because of my wife's request that the twins learn about God. I continued my substance abuse, even though I had toned it down considerably. We were much like any other family, with the exception of my abusive outburst after drinking too much.

We were trying to get back on our feet and slowly started paying off outstanding debt that we incurred when I walked away from the business. I was beginning to see the light at the end of the tunnel. And remember what I said earlier about money giving us a false sense of security? I had gone by the bank's ATM to withdraw some cash and my card was confiscated and I had a message to see one of the bank officers. When I went inside, I was told that all of my accounts, personal and business, had been levied by the IRS for back taxes. This was the calm before the storm, financially and literally.

It was Labor Day weekend 2004, and Hurricane Francis was heading right for us. We did what everyone does—board up the windows, buy water, food, and batteries, and hope for the best. I have been through dozens of hurricanes and, quite honestly, never considered them a major threat because you were always given several days warning. That feeling of false security was about to change.

My wife and twins went to stay with our neighbor who had small children of their own, and Kevin went to stay with his girlfriend. It was just me and our dog, Cody. I will never forget that sound that the winds make when you are getting pounded. It sounds like a locomotive is on your roof. **"And suddenly there came a sound from heaven, as of a rushing mighty wind, and it filled the whole house where they were sitting"** (Acts 2:2).

I was sitting in darkness (literally and spiritually) on the living room floor when the ceiling began to fall and then remembered earlier in the day when I commented that someone had lost his roof wind turbines; it was me. I moved to the bathtub in the older section of the house, our eighty-pound dog and I inside the tub with a mattress over us. After hours of worrying and getting pounded by the other side of the hurricane, it was finally over. **"Which of you by worrying can add one cubit to his stature"** (Matthew 6:27)?

We went outside, and I was happy to see that my family was fine. I remember thinking how awesome it was how people get together and help one another during a time like this. There was no electricity, no cell service, no way to cook inside the house, no running water, no available ATMs or anywhere to purchase provisions, none of the modern-day conveniences that we take for granted every day.

One of our neighbors started making several pots of coffee from his Coleman stove, another was making breakfast for anyone who was hungry, and several neighbors huddled together in prayer and thanked God for His protection. As I began to assess the damage, I was amazed how much damage there was to the new addition of the house. The entire exterior wall that framed the new bedrooms and bathroom was completely destroyed and had suffered major water damage. The older section of the home which was built close to fifty years ago was undamaged, with the exception of the ceiling because of the rain that was entering through the roof opening.

The water in the swimming pool was black, and debris from neighboring homes were everywhere. We spent the next few days cleaning up, and the eleven wheelbarrows of roof shingles that I removed from the pool with my feet is something that I will never forget. The small town that we live in was at a standstill. The landfills were closed, and there was no trash removal for several weeks.

We spent the next several days trying to survive without the modern-day conveniences that I mentioned earlier. There are so many of God's blessings that we don't ever really think about and appreciate, until they are no longer available—no indoor plumbing, no way to do laundry, no ice, no cold anything, no TV. And how much canned tuna and chicken can you eat?

There was also a mandatory curfew in effect which is enforced by local and county law enforcement where you are not allowed to leave your property from sunset to sunrise because of looting. You are not allowed to take a walk, visit a neighbor, or drive anywhere. I understand the importance of this ordinance, but it felt like martial law to me. My family's security was not an issue or concern to me; being told I couldn't go anywhere or leave my property was.

It finally dawned on me that the towns forty miles further south were barely affected by the hurricane. I took every cooler I could find and visited the grocery store in Fort Lauderdale. I have never been so excited to visit a deli and eat hot food that was just prepared. What do they say about going shopping when you are hungry? I spent over three hundred dollars, and I am forever grateful to the young man at Dunkin' Donuts who allowed me to take as much ice as I wanted. Being able to share the prepared foods and ice with family and neighbors was a joyful feeling.

After two weeks, our electricity was restored, and we began to get back to some type of normal living again when we were told that Hurricane Jeannie now strengthened to a category four and was heading straight for us. There was no way I was going to put my family through that again. We loaded up both our vehicles and reserved a large chalet, and all of us went to Gatlinburg and stayed there until the storm had passed. Yes, we took Cody.

When we returned home, there was even more damage, and the swimming pool was again filled with roof shingles but was only seven wheelbarrows this time! Say what you will about the Walton's, but they gave all of their employees who were affected by the hurricanes several hundred dollars. My wife was able to return to work, but the majority of my clients were insurance companies, and after several months, I had to face the fact that I was out of business.

Our homeowners insurance company paid us close to a hundred thousand dollars for the damage, which was an enormous blessing, but we were so far behind on our bills and now had 75 percent of our earnings gone. I tried finding work, but quite honestly, I was tired of the investigative biz.

We used the money to live which also forced me to perform the repairs myself. I have never been a Handy Andy, but I had no choice but to learn what I didn't know. This was not a few small repairs; it was an entire thirty-four-foot weight-bearing wall that had to be removed and replaced, among hundreds of other projects, not to mention the black mold that was now also living with us. The repairs took me close to a year and was the reason that I suffered physical injuries.

During 2005 and within one week, both our vehicles were repossessed due to outstanding debt that we had when I walked away from the business back in '99, even though we had clear titles. We were able to secure a vehicle through her father, and he held the paper, but we were now limited to only one. Several weeks later, we were informed that one of our creditors was legally going to garish my wife's wages. I took a position with a local agency as a field investigator but several months later, they could not provide me with sufficient wages to meet our budget.

One of the good things about having free time was that I started thinking about all of my mother's recipes and the ones that I had created. All of my older kids also like to cook, so I decided to make a cookbook for each of them with about thirty-five recipes, and I can only hope that they truly enjoy having them available. Will they survive time and be available to their children when they get older?

I could no longer ignore the severe pain that I was experiencing, and I started treating with an orthopedic surgeon who diagnosed me with two torn rotator cuffs and severe damage to my neck. He suggested surgery, but after learning that our share of the expenses would be several thousand dollars, I declined because we were sinking fast financially. Looking back, I found a short-term solution but also created a very long-term problem.

This was when my addiction to pain pills began. I would lay in bed for twenty hours a day and watch television and was a poor excuse for a human being. My wife worked full time, and we lived mostly off of the remainder of the insurance money. My attitude was terrible, and how my family put up with me must have been patience sent from God. I did not contribute anything and basically lived for the drugs. I would take twice the suggested dosage, pig out, and sleep for the next several hours.

That pattern continued day after day, week after week, and month after month. I lost so much of the precious times with my twins because they were ten years old and involved in so many school, church, and other activities. My wife showed unbelievable love, grace, and mercy toward me, and for that, I am forever grateful.

The following summer, I could not continue living this way and made the decision to stop taking the Rx and just live with the pain. It was my forty-ninth birthday.

It was day four, and Katie called and told me that the kids were staying later at school and that I would need to go to the school because they would need a parent there to release them. I know this does not sound like a big deal, but I would need to either walk or ride my bike the half mile to the school. Again not a big deal, unless you are too weak to even walk to the kitchen. I ended up riding my bike in the summer heat, and when my neighbor saw me, she laughed and said I looked like death.

I was able to wean myself off of the Rx and began to live with the pain. After getting a second vehicle, I took a job as a field investigator with a local agency, and I began to feel somewhat normal again.

Within several months, I resumed my dependency on narcotics but tried not to abuse the dosage. Like I said before, the bad thing about taking a dangerous narcotic is that your body builds a tolerance to them, and no matter how hard you try, your dosage will increase over time.

I began to realize that the real estate values in our area were worth twice as much as only a few years before. Considering all of the financial problems we were having and my wife not really happy about her wages being garnished, refinancing our current mortgage seemed to be a suitable option. Once again, I tried fixing a short-term problem but created a larger one.

We were able to remove over a hundred thousand dollars in equity and satisfied the majority of our creditors. We were very happy that we were able to pay off existing debt, but this quick fix had just doubled our mortgage, again.

The following summer, my employer had a slow month, and we missed a mortgage payment. The lender was less than cooperative in allowing us to defer one payment, and we were informed that if we did not become current, the property would go into foreclosure.

In late July 2008, we were forced to vacate the property, and quite honestly, it broke my heart. This was the house that I grew up in, the neighborhood that all five of my children played in and where we called home. God later helped me realize that leaving was actually a blessing. My father and brother both physically died inside the property.

I found a beautiful rental near the beach, but the rent was close to the mortgage payment that we could not afford! Once again, Isaiah tried to tell me that we could not afford this home but, well, you should know my destructive behavior by now. Four months after moving into the rental, my employer went out of business, and our financial problems would be resolved by my wife and His endless grace. Katie secured a second job, and our landlord blessed us by reducing our rent by 50 percent with the agreement that I would perform some repairs and was now obligated for all further repairs and maintenance.

In April 2009, I was able to find employment, and even though it did not pay much, I was just happy to be out of the investigative business. This position was during the third shift and allowed me to drive and pick up the twins from school and help out at home.

Later that year, Katie's father had become very ill and was suffering from COPD. She flew to Michigan and was able to spend a few days with him before he was called home. I always liked her father and can only hope that he is with the Lord.

Now having to perform physical labor at work, my consummation of opiates began to double within only a few months. I know doctors have their patient's best interest at heart, but how can you continue to prescribe hundreds of Rx per month and then ask your patient if they have a drug problem!

In January, I visited my doctor for my monthly appointment, and it appeared to be like any other visit, until I was asked to give a urine sample. When I asked if this was for all his patients or just me, he replied, "Just you!" Within a few weeks, I received a certified letter from his office terminating our doctor-patient agreement because of unapproved narcotics.

That was when I started to panic and began doctor shopping and visiting "pill mills." What was previously affordable had now begun to cost me ten times the cost per month for appointments and illegal street buys. I continued my abusive lifestyle, and every month, I found myself taking more and more pills. My destructive behavior was out of control, and my relationships got worse because of my selfish attitude and addiction.

Congrats! You made it through the first fifty-plus years of my selfish carnal life. Let's now talk about what is important, what God has done in my life during the last few years.

CHAPTER 8

The Corruptible Seed Is Crushed

And I will put enmity between you and the woman and between your seed and her seed; He shall bruise your head, and you shall bruise His heel.
—**Genesis 3:15**

It was Thursday, February 10, 2011, and I began to come out of my spiritual coma. I will not go into great detail but feel as though the following few sentences need to be said. The rest of the afternoon and evening, I became consumed with evil thoughts and cannot even put into print what I was thinking. I paced the floor for several hours and prayed and meditated for Him to help me.

I am sure that there is a medical term for taking ten pills a day to none, but it feels like death, so why wouldn't Satan be present? I thanked God for allowing me to live, and He allowed me to believe that there was a glimmer of hope.

A few days later, I left the house and went to the local market. It was the first time I had really gone outside in over ten days. The air was sweeter, the grass was greener, and my views and attitude seemed better. I realized that I was still under the influence of the Rx, but something was different.

I had humbly accepted Christ; I was now a child of God. I was redeemed by His sacred blood and the power of the cross. **"I have been crucified with Christ; it is no longer I who live, but Christ** lives in me; and the life which I now live in the flesh, I live by faith in the Son of God, who loved me and gave Himself for me" (Galatians 2:20).

While sitting in the car, I began crying and thanking God for giving me another chance. When I returned home, Katie asked me if I had smoked because my eyes were red, and I looked different. When I tried to explain what I was feeling, I began crying uncontrollably and could not even speak. This feeling lasted over an hour, and I remember it like it was five minutes ago.

I later began wondering if I had received the baptism of the Holy Spirit. I knew that with/in/through Christ, my life would never be the same. **"Therefore, if anyone is in Christ, he is a new creation; old things have passed away; behold, all things have become new" (2 Corinthians 5:17).**

During the next few weeks, I began to really enjoy my life and the things that I used to avoid and complain about. This was a very special time for me because it allowed me to spend several hours a day getting to know the Lord.

I remember one afternoon, I was listening to Sid Roth's supernatural show about a man who had experienced God's transition by faith. This man was in the bathroom in LAX and needed to get to London for a family emergency but did not have the funds. He was a godly man and had spent the majority of his life doing mission work overseas and was now arguing with God because he felt abandoned.

God asked him if he believed He was who He said He was. The man agreed, and he was told to leave the bathroom. When he did, he walked out of the bathroom and was in the airport in London!

Anyway, after seeing this show, I began to realize that anything was possible through the Father, if it would glorify Him and His kingdom. I walked into the garage to have a cigarette and remember thinking that this was a feel-good story, but how did I know if it was really true? **"While we do not look at the things which are seen, but at the things which are not seen. For the things which are seen are temporary, but the things which are not seen are eternal" (2 Corinthians 4:18).** I thought to myself the same thing that millions of others have thought, wish there was a sign.

At that exact moment, the door leading from the garage into the laundry room flew open, slammed against the wall, and the Holy Spirit said, "Faith." It was not that I doubted the power of the Lord, but I had just received confirmation from God Almighty, and His words freaked me out a little.

A few days later, I contacted my nephew who was now a youth minister, and he agreed to meet me for breakfast later in the week. I had written down dozens of questions that I had, and he blessed me by spending several hours with me.

The first was that the Christian race is a marathon, not a sprint. The second was that although good deeds and works are important, it is not about your knowledge of the Word but is all about having a personal relationship with Jesus Christ. He explained it this way to me. How do you get to know someone? By spending time with them (praying) and listening to what they have to say (reading the Bible). Thank you, Michael. You have earned heavenly treasures for what you did for me.

I spent several hours a day praying and reading the Bible and became obsessed with trying to memorize Bible stories and verses. During my studies, I realized that I am the type of person who remembers much more of what I write than what I read. My solution, I started hand writing the books of Matthew and John, which may not seem like a big deal, but try to appreciate that I was reading the amplified version!

I was trying to build a strong spiritual foundation. **"Therefore whoever hears these sayings of Mine, and does them, I will liken him to a wise man who built his house on the rock" (Matthew 7:24).** I knew that I was in a marathon, and over time, God has taught me that our ending means more than our beginning.

Looking back at this time period, I was truly living in the Spirit. I remember thinking how clear everything seemed, and nothing else mattered but God. I actually felt guilty wondering how nonbelievers got through the day. I now also realize it is very easy to get complacent over time and lose this heavenly gift, if we do not stay close to God.

Still having the physical injuries that got me into this mess, my sister-in-law Judy told me about a friend that lived in North Carolina who has the anointed power of healing through Jesus Christ. I told her that I wanted to learn more about spiritual healing and having the faith to receive it.

In early March, Katie called me from work and asked me if one of my best friends from back in the day had a grandson because he had recently died. I searched the local paper and confirmed that it was in fact my friends Kevin and Audrey, whom I had only seen a few times in the past thirty years.

They had recently returned to South Florida after being out of state for two-plus decades. I contacted him, and when he told me how their first grandson had passed, I was speechless. I will not go into any further details except to say that the prince of this world had his hands in his death, and the child's mother and new boyfriend are in prison.

I wanted to attend the funeral and hopefully try to comfort them, but what can you say at a time like this? I just knew what not to say. Having buried my entire family, I always found it odd that people always say "they are in a better place now." Even though this may or may not be true, it is of little comfort for those who are grieving. Just love on them and tell them that you are here if they need you. Without a follow up weeks later when it usually hits them, your words will fall on deaf ears.

I asked God to give me the strength to comfort my friends because my ego and pride were a barrier because of my appearance. My business suit and haircut could not hide the fact that I was missing several teeth and very self-conscious when around others.

Through His strength, I decided to attend, and when I saw this beautiful boy laid to rest, I could not control my emotions. God had truly softened my heart because I had never even met this small child and don't recall crying when my own family died. It was nice seeing them after so many years, but I began thinking about what Kevin and his family must be going through.

I remember asking God why things like this happen, but all things are revealed in time. Kevin and I hung out every day when we were teens, and he had asked me to be his best man when they got married over thirty years ago. I remained for about an hour and felt bad that I didn't attend the burial or get together later, but my pride and ego stole my peace because of my appearance.

Several days later, my oldest daughter, Kristy, called and told me that she was pregnant. Even though my first thought was a legalistic and religious one because I thought that they were putting the cart before the horse, God quickly reminded me that children are a gift from him, and His blessings are not to be questioned. I felt so blessed that my daughter was giving me my first grandchild, and I began to wonder about the saying "One is born when one is taken."

I wanted to get involved in a grace-filled church and started attending the church where my nephew was the youth pastor. I was now completely clean from the Rx which was not by my hand but by His. The first service I attended, I knew I was in a good place because their mission statement is "No perfect people allowed." The pastor is a very powerful speaker and someone that you enjoy listening to.

I made the decision to get baptized at the beach on Easter Sunday. I asked my entire family to attend the morning service with me, and much to my surprise, they agreed. The majority of my family are like most people when it comes to attending church; they are CEOs (Christmas/Easter only).

When the pastor instructed anyone who wanted to surrender their life to Christ to come forward, Kevin and Kristy looked at each other with a curious spirit, and I may have missed a divine opportunity when I did not take them by the hand for the altar call.

Later that day, Johnny and I were baptized at the beach, and that was a truly spiritual moment. The senior pastor baptized me, and my nephew Michael baptized Johnny. I will always remember that feeling when I went under the water. It was as if God had slowed down time. That 2–3 seconds seemed like an hour. **"But, beloved, do not forget this one thing, that with the Lord one day is as a thousand years, and a thousand years as one day" (2 Peter 3:8).**

I continued my daily time with God and His messages, and while reading one of Paul's many Epistles, God spoke to me through His word when I saw the verse in 2 Thessalonians 3:10 that says, "For even when we were with you, we commanded you this: If anyone will not work, neither shall he eat." I tried to dismiss this verse but began feeling guilty because I was not working.

I spent the next several weeks trying to find a job, even though my wife was content with working two jobs because I took care of the kids and also the house. I soon realized that being in my midfifties and being a convicted felon was going to be an uphill battle. Don't you hate filling out applications and updating a resume when it all seems in vain?

After earning some money doing odd jobs, I decided to do something nice for the kids and took them bowling. A few minutes after we arrived, I saw a girl that I had not seen in over thirty years. She was a good friend of Sue's, and I had always thought that she was a very special person.

As I began talking with her, I felt led to tell her my personal testimony regarding my substance abuse and being born-again. She told me that her husband also suffered from substance abuse and was trying to get clean. She asked if I would talk to him about my experiences and how I found Jesus.

Her husband and I spoke for several minutes, and two years later, I ran into her, and she told me that her husband was now clean and had surrendered his life to Christ and was trying to help others by telling them about Christ through his personal experiences and testimony. I felt so blessed that God helped him and that I might have played a very small part.

When we finished bowling, I saw my sister-in-law, Cheryl, yes, the one that I kicked out of my mother's house after my brother's death. I had only seen her a few times in the last twenty years, and she had now remarried. We talked for over an hour, and I am happy to say that she has once again become a big part of my life.

During the last several months, I had been suffering from severe dental pain, and no longer being a slave to narcotics, I usually just tried to pray the pain away. Sometimes it worked; sometimes it didn't. The point is that I could no longer ignore the pain and/or my self-conscious appearance.

I started calling several local offices that accepted our insurance, and the best estimate I could get was about four thousand dollars for the complete procedure. Our cost would be about twelve hundred dollars. We certainly did not have that kind of money, and Katie called her mother and asked her for a loan. Even after all of the problems I had created for her daughter, she blessed me by saying yes.

Remember the handwritten pages I was writing from the book of Matthew and John? Well, I had finally finished and wanted to back up my writings, so I had Johnny and Megan type what I had written onto the computer. They were not thrilled about this, but subconsciously, they were learning the Gospel without ever having to read the Bible. This went on for several months and turned out to be close to one hundred typed pages. I continued praying for some type of spiritual dream to show me what I was supposed to be doing regarding my faith and works.

I began to realize that I had empathy in my heart for the homeless and the needy, you know, the least of these. I guess it was because I was very close to living with them if it had not been for my wife and how seriously she took our wedding vows.

I was sitting home one afternoon reading the Word, and He put this on my heart: *Could I do more for those less fortunate than myself?* For the next few days, I continued thinking about what I would do for others if I had money and why He put this thought into my head.

A few days later, I visited my post office box, which I had not done in several weeks, and what I saw was amazing. There was a check for me for one hundred dollars from a customer I used to have on my route. The check said "Happy Holidays." It was now the end of July! Was that God using someone to bless others or just a strange coincidence? You decide.

I cashed the check and went to the dollar store to purchase personal hygiene items, bottled waters, and other much needed items. My plan was to make bags for the needy and bless them through His provisions, although I did spend about ten dollars on myself.

I started driving through the downtown areas and, much to my surprise, could not find any homeless people because the city was trying to clean up the area. I found one older gentleman pushing a shopping cart through a low-income high-crime area. He would not talk to me at first but seemed happy when he saw the provisions. I certainly felt out of my comfort zone and, quite honestly, started to wonder what I was doing there. I began thinking about how I would react if the roles were reversed. God gave me a calming and joyful feeling as I sat in the nearby grass and just hung out. When I was leaving, he looked at me and said, "God bless you."

On my way home, I was driving near the old neighborhood and saw someone in a shopping plaza holding a cardboard sign and several people standing around him. He was holding a sign that said, "Will pray with you for something to eat." The people around him were all praying with him, and I noticed that they had bought him a large bag of food from McDonald's.

I did not stay that day, but over the next several months, I got to know him, brought him some provisions, and often prayed with him. He ended up getting a job for a fitness gym within the plaza, holding a street sign advertisement. Several months later, he purchased a vehicle and has not been seen since. Was he a troubled young man or a prophet of the Lord?

After leaving the plaza, I saw large lettering on a vehicle that covered the entire rear glass. As I got closer, I was so happy to see that it said, "If you were on trial for being a Christian, would there be enough evidence to convict you?" We ended up at the light together and I gave him a big thumbs-up.

That is one of the things that I love most of our Living God. Really think about what He did in a short period of time. I tried to help a homeless man; He allowed me to meet another homeless man and saw an out-of-the-box Christian message in a period of maybe forty-five minutes.

It was time to address my dental issues. I found an office and had two visits to be fitted for the dentures, and even though I gagged when they put that clay mold into my mouth, I knew that I had to do it. Remember earlier when I said that faith was one of my spiritual gifts? Well, for several months, I had prayed that I would wake up with new teeth. I knew God could do anything, but I didn't understand how God really works. He always requires our involvement.

Katie drove me to my appointment, and we said a prayer before entering the office. I found myself in that reclining chair that I had been avoiding for over ten years. Katie remained in the room with me until the dentist started putting his knee on my chest to extract the last few. The procedure took over two hours, and after three dozen shots of Novocain and having sixteen teeth extracted at one time, *it was finished.* The only thing that got me through this was thinking about Jesus and how He suffered on the cross, and my pain was nothing compared to what He did for us.

During the last several months, Megan had been visiting a girlfriend in a neighborhood that I was not thrilled about, and she repeatedly reminded me that it was not her friend's fault that her parents were not up to my standards. I soon discovered that my daughter was lying to us and was actually visiting her boyfriend that lived in the same neighborhood on an adjacent street.

When we sat down to talk, I had a hundred questions but had to pray for wisdom and peace because my flesh was trying to control my spirit; no one likes being lied to. She told me that I was not going to like what she had to say, but I had no idea what was coming.

She said that she had been dating a nineteen-year-old guy that she had met at work, and that was the good news. He was unemployed, lived with his "bros," did not have a car, quit school when he was fifteen, had been arrested several times, was currently on probation, used to be in a gang, and might sell drugs! Remember earlier when I said people don't really surprise me anymore? This was beyond a surprise. Megan was only fifteen years old.

I had learned a valuable lesson with Kristy when she went through her rebellious stage a decade earlier. The bottom line is that being strict and a controlling parent only adds to the problems, if you did not take the time and effort to raise them with godly truths, and even then, it's a crapshoot. The more I disciplined her, the more she rebelled, and being unable to physically control her, there is not much you can do except give it to God.

Those of you reading this with your imaginary children have been misled. I have talked to dozens of people who all said the same thing—"I would not allow my child to control my life"—which is good in theory, but when I asked them how they would control their child, none of them could tell me. It is not illegal for a child to run away from home, and a problem child at home trumps a dead child on the streets.

After thinking and praying about Megan's choices, I asked her to bring him by so I could meet him. How bad could he be? I grew up and hung around with some real characters. He was not as bad as I thought; he was much worse. Our daughter is beautiful, and this young man could not look you in the eyes if his life depended on it. I sat down with him and told him that I would not judge him because of his appearance and expected the same in return.

After thirty minutes, I realized that this young man was a product of his environment and had been on his own for several years. He is the type of young man that God may use some day and have an extremely powerful testimony and help bring others to Christ. Regardless, I did not want my daughter dating him, but she could move in with him tomorrow, and there would not be a thing I could do about it.

I asked him if he would be interested in attending church with us. You would have thought that I just asked him for a kidney. He told me that he had never been to a church and did not think he would fit in. I told him that God loves everyone regardless of their appearance, beliefs, and actions. A few days later, my daughter must have been talking to him about church because he said he would go with us the following Sunday.

I should have remembered that he said that he had never been to a church. When we went to pick him up, he was wearing saggy jeans, a torn shirt, and a ball cap that he wore backward. There was nothing I could say. I had told him that God did not care about his appearance, even though I knew that people generally do.

The sermon was unusually flat that day, and I truly expected him to bolt from his seat because he kept looking at the door. When the service was over, I asked him what he thought. He said it was not as bad as he had imagined; it was much worse. That was the only time he attended with us.

CHAPTER 9

Getting Involved with the Body of Christ

I continued praying for a grace-filled church that was somewhat close to the house because of the condition of my car. What God provided may blow your mind, and remember what I said earlier about not believing in coincidences.

Since the girls were working, Johnny and I ended up going together, and the church service was held in what I can only describe as a movie-theater stadium-type setting, with a coffee, juice, and pastry bar. This was quite different from most churches I had attended, but there was a positive spiritual energy in the building.

As I was listening to the pastor, I kept thinking that I knew him, which is not a stretch when you live somewhere for a long period of time. I realized that I used to play baseball with him forty-plus years ago, and his father was our coach and noticed him in the front row.

As I began to think about this time in my life, I realized that I was not very fond of him or his father, even though they were always nice to me. I remembered attending a First Baptist Church youth group outing when I was in seventh grade, and his father was one of the group leaders.

Anyway, when the service was over, I wanted to say hello and see if the pastor remembered me. I was standing in the shadows waiting my turn because he was talking with a young woman, and several people were in front of me. The young woman turned around, and it was Grace's mother, my girlfriend from when I was seventeen who

I had not seen in over thirty years! I was speechless. Those negative memories and feelings hit me hard. Would she even talk to me? Would she blame me? How did our relationship end?

I told Johnny that I used to date her in high school, and he laughed, saying, "She will not remember you. You are old and fat. You know how teenagers are."

Well, it turned out that my son was right. She looked right at me and kept walking. She was not ignoring me; she really did not recognize me, until I called her by her high school nickname.

She looked at me and smiled and said, "OMG, this is the last place I would ever expect to see you. You didn't burst into flames when you entered the church?"

I laughed and guess that I deserve that.

We ignored the elephant in the room and just tried to catch up because she also had her teenage child with her. She had lived a rough life, due to no fault of her own. Her mother and husband had recently passed away, and she was recovering from brain surgery. I told her about my family, and even though it was very awkward, it was nice seeing her again. I began thinking that I had mixed emotions about the possibility of seeing her on a weekly basis.

The senior pastor did not recognize me, but after I told him my name, he started telling his friends what a fast runner and all-star I was. Honestly, it was a little embarrassing. We were never as good as the stories that are told years later.

I started getting involved with this church and their outreach programs. The first one that I ever attended was for the homeless at a church that was located in the downtown area. I was amazed at how much they really seemed to listen to the message and how they were no different from me; they just didn't have a beautiful wife to support them. Some of them suffered from mental health issues, but most of them were just hungry and wanted to feel loved.

The volunteers who had been doing this for a while treated them like equals and knew all of them by name. That was huge to me because you can't receive respect if you don't give it. When I left that evening, they allowed me to take a few take-out containers which I gave to two of my homeless friends after I found them. I attended this outreach program several times, and on one evening, my oldest son, Kevin, came with me and was truly blessed by His peace and joy.

Our church was having a brunch for their *next* class, in efforts to educate people about the Gospel and convey to them their spiritual gifts. I had met the guy who ran the coffee shop and organized the Thanksgiving dinner and learned that he and his wife have an outreach ministry that feeds the homeless a hot breakfast once a month.

I decided to volunteer my time and arrived at the church around 5:00 a.m., and we prepared food for forty people at the church and also for the outreach breakfast. It was a pleasure doing something that was for His glory and His kingdom. The volunteers were awesome, and I am happy to say that I have built eternal friendships with many of them.

During the next few weeks, I kept thinking about that verse in 2 Thessalonians, and I knew it was God's way of telling me to return to work. It had been eight months. In my heart, I knew that I had to contribute, but what really bothered me was giving up my special time with the Lord, just to earn money. Welcome to planet Earth!

I continued praying on what I should do, and then I had a dream about my prior boss whom I ended up in litigation with a dozen years ago. What! There was no way that I was going to crawl back to him and beg for a job. Was this the dream that I had been praying for?

There is a reason that they refer to the Word as the Living Bible. Within a few days, it seemed like everywhere I looked I kept seeing the verse **"And whoever exalts himself will be abased, and he who humbles himself will be exalted"** (Matthew 23:12).

I knew what I had to do, and after a few days, I contacted my ex-partner, which was very difficult, to say the least. Try to understand and appreciate that this was not just some business partnership that had gone south. He was the one who gave me my start in the industry. He had been my mentor, he was Kevin's godfather, my best man in my current marriage, and a good friend for over twenty years.

The good Lord had also softened his heart during the last decade, and his kind words were a comfort and a blessing to me. The following week, we had a meeting, and both of us agreed that we both did not handle our fallout very well. We talked for close to two hours, and quite honestly, it felt like our past was just that, our past. He welcomed me back and even helped out financially to get me back to work.

I realized that taking a step of faith and doing what is not comfortable in the flesh is maybe how He molds us. At this time in my life, I really disliked doing surveillance, but you do what you know, and besides, it always paid very well. Getting used to sitting in a car for fifty hours a week again was a blessing and a curse.

I contacted my sister-in-law Judy and told her that I was ready to talk to her friend in North Carolina regarding my physical issues. I had never talked to him before, and after a few minutes, I realized that this godly man was anointed and knew how to deliver the healing power and authority of God the Father, through Jesus Christ.

I followed his instructions and repeated his words and prayers. When I was told to hold my shoulder with my opposite hand, he repeatedly said "In Jesus's name, in Jesus's name," and I felt a tingling in my shoulder like when your foot is asleep. This did not remove my pain like we would imagine, but within a few days, I realized that my neck and shoulders no longer hurt. Thank You, Jesus.

My oldest daughter, Kristy, and PJ had planned a huge baby shower and get together at one of the pavilions at the beach and had over a hundred people in attendance. Although this was a joyous event, I was now confronted by my ex-wife and her parents who treated me like poison.

A few months ago, I had anticipated our paths crossing, and since my ex-wife and I don't seem to get along, I decided to write a letter to her parents. I basically told them that I loved and respected them and asked for their forgiveness for leaving their daughter and whatever else I might have done. This infuriated Ann.

I have found that when you are in a negative situation and confronted with emotional hardship, you have two choices: one, you can be petty, evil and condescending, or have the heart of Christ and just love on. Thanks to God, I was the latter.

The church was beginning to organize its Bible studies and/or growth groups, and the woman in charge of these groups is someone whose spirit just captures you and warrants involvement. I attended my first growth group, and I was extremely nervous because I did not really know anyone. Most of these people were my age but were very successful financially.

They asked me if I would like to share anything about myself, and they may have regretted asking me that question. I talked for about twenty minutes, giving my personal testimony, and they did not judge me, just showed me compassion and love.

I remained involved with this group for several months, and when the next group was forming, I was asked to colead the meeting. They must have seen something in me that only the good Lord could have shown them.

I have always struggled with a consistent prayer life, considering how most of us think about prayer. I am the type who tries to talk to God throughout the day as opposed to sitting down at specific times, even though I do try to start everyday with scripture or writing in my journal.

Thanksgiving week was here, and our church was planning an outreach dinner and asked for volunteers to cook the holiday meal for approximately four hundred people. I showed up at the church at 4:00 a.m., and my wife and the twins showed up a little later. We cooked 35–40 turkeys, two hundred pounds of potatoes, a few gallons of gravy, all of the other traditional dishes, and twenty pounds of fruit salad. I have always felt good about helping others, but if your heart is not in the right place, you are just feeding your flesh and your own desires.

During the second week of December, Kristy went into the hospital to get ready for the baby, and most of the family was there, including my ex-wife. After a few hours, we were told that the baby was not ready yet and that they would induce labor if she didn't deliver within twenty-four hours. She allowed me to say a prayer with her, and I asked God to bless her and my granddaughter.

We returned the following afternoon, and I could tell that my daughter was upset. She had just been told that the baby was breech, and they would need to do a C-section. Medically, this was not a big deal, but Isaiah had told me the day before that she would need to have a C-section. My oldest son, Kevin, who may suffer from anxiety attacks, became very nervous, and he allowed me to lay hands on him and offer him a healing prayer through Jesus Christ. He said that it helped.

At 5:35 pm., my daughter delivered a beautiful baby girl, and both were in good health. It took me several days to realize that I was a grandfather. My family, my ex-wife and her new husband, and her parents were all celebrating together. Only God could do that.

We spent Christmas Eve with my sister-in-law Judy and her husband, Michael, in Vero Beach and had a wonderful evening. They later told us that they were planning a surprise birthday party for his father's eightieth birthday within a few weeks.

After the holiday, Megan had told me that she was not really getting along with her boyfriend lately because of his attitude and lifestyle. I told her that sometimes that is how relationships work out. It is always easy to have joy when its new and exciting, but true love is built over time and tribulations, not by being intimate.

I had told her before my idea of true love. You have just been married and are driving to your honeymoon when your spouse suffers a spinal injury and will be paralyzed and bedridden for the rest of his life. You are expected to be the caregiver and surrender your entire life for them. What would you do? Are you willing to surrender your life for another? Kind of what Jesus did—true agape love.

Kevin had recently told me that PJ's mother had been recently complaining about health problems and had now slipped into a coma and was currently in hospice at a local hospital. I had seen her for years at the local store but never knew it was his mother until recently.

A few days later, I was told that she passed away, and everyone got together afterward to celebrate her life, and my ex-wife asked me in front of everyone if my fifteen-year-old daughter was dating a nineteen-year-old. I tried not to be a jerk, but I said, "No, he is now twenty!" All I could do was smile and say yes as she made me look like a fool.

With the new year here, I began to really evaluate my love for the Lord and my motives for what I was doing. On a positive note,

I was clean, my relationships were improving, I was employed, but something was bothering me. It took me several weeks to figure it out and through His guidance and wisdom, I finally did.

I had become a Bible-thumping legalistic Pharisee! I had gotten caught up in works, serving and trying to act and look holy. I had forgotten where I came from and who I was just a year ago, I was the corruptible seed who tried to kill myself with drugs at a hotel. Now I am judging others just because they did not have my zeal for Christ.

I spent the majority of my time thinking and praying about my behavior and continued searching for my purpose without pissing everyone off. One of the problems of being an extremist is trying to find a suitable balance. I realized that I needed to surrender all to Christ!

Have you ever heard that everyone is either in a spiritual storm, coming out of a storm, or about to enter one? Things were going very well, and that should have been my first clue. For the last several days, I had felt an uneasiness in my spirit, and looking back, there were various signs, but the **busyness** of life blinds us.

Toward the end of January, I was in the garage when I heard Megan getting sick in the bathroom. When I asked her what was wrong, she told me that something she ate must have made her sick. I drove them to school, and when I got home, I started cleaning up the house since it was my day off.

When I started cleaning her bathroom, I noticed a brown paper bag at the bottom of the waste basket. I opened the bag and saw three used pregnancy tests. I was speechless and terrified. She was not a problem child, but we were concerned about her and her relationship with her boyfriend. I knew in my heart at that moment that she was pregnant and should have not been so naive. I spent the majority of the day praying and looking for discernment from the Holy Spirit, but my carnal thoughts and nature was a barrier between us.

When I picked up the kids from school, we talked like we did every day, and in a loving but firm tone I asked her if there was any-thing she wanted to tell me. She looked at me with her big beautiful eyes that were now tearing up and said, "I'm pregnant!"

The next ten seconds, I felt rage like I had not felt in several years. The Holy Spirit had to remind me that she was being honest with me and needed my love and forgiveness, not a raging parent that felt betrayed by lies and deceit. She had not done anything that I had not done.

By the look on Johnny's face, she had not told him either, and she later told me that she had not told her mother. When we got home, I had to excuse myself for a few minutes to compose myself and process my thoughts.

When I returned, she was on the phone with her boyfriend, and I told her that I wanted to talk to him, but I guess he was too busy wrapping up blues. I asked her what her plan was, and I knew what she was going to say before she finished her sentence. I told her that abortion was not an option, and there was no way that she was going to murder a child. She told me that it was her boyfriend who had made the suggestion to get an abortion, and he asked her if she had the money for the procedure! What a stand-up guy! I had heard enough! I told her that I loved her and not to worry because her mother and I were here to help her, not punish her.

I don't know if I really believe that but she needed to hear it. Megan was scared, emotional and clueless of what she had done. I say that after knowing the headaches and hardships of raising small children.

I prayed for several days on what I should do and it was now time to address another problem, namely her boyfriend. I sat down with Megan and tried to explain to her that she was at a crossroad in her young life. If she remained with this young man her life might be an uphill struggle.

I had visions of her being in her midtwenties working two full-time jobs with several kids, while he sat home watching TV and selling drugs. That was when she told me that they had been discussing moving in together and playing house while my wife and I paid all the bills. When pigs fly!

I was trying to reason with a teenager's mind and hormones, and I was losing. The voice of truth stepped in, and together we took a different approach. If she wanted to struggle her entire life, that was one thing, but was it fair to her child? Did she want her child to be ashamed of her parents? Did she really think that her boyfriend would be a good husband and father?

I told her point-blank that we loved her, but there was no way her boyfriend would ever live here. If she made the decision to move out of the house, she was on her own. I know that sounds callous and unloving, but that is what she needed to hear.

She began to see the big picture, and one of her spiritual gifts has always been a loving heart and compassion for children. She finally told me that her biggest concern was that her child would grow up without a daddy. I told you she was practical and loving. I explained to her that her family was behind her. I asked her to trust me, which was not easy because of my past, but God allowed her to take a step of faith and put her future into our hands.

They had made a decision to act like adults, and now it was my turn. She was going to end her relationship with her boyfriend immediately and have no further contact with him. I informed her that I was going to have a talk with him, and he would have no further contact with her. If either one of them breached the agreement, then I would have no choice but to have him arrested for statutory rape because he was an adult and had impregnated a fifteen-year-old. I told her that it was not my intention or desire to send him to prison, but considering he was still on probation, he would do serious time. She reluctantly agreed but knew that I was not joking.

I had to pray and meditate for wisdom and guidance before calling her boyfriend because I did not want my prior self and anger to control my thoughts and words. Through the Holy Spirit, I was very calm and relaxed and explained to him that until he got his life together and was serious about being a father, he was not to have any further contact with my daughter. If he truly loved her and wanted a child, he would get a job, look into getting his GED and a vehicle.

He actually listened to me, but then told me if I wanted my grandchild to grow up without a father, then so be it. I tried to be a father figure for him because that was what had been missing in most of his adolescence and adult life. He also told me that he was not interested in getting a job and would not be financially obligated to my daughter and/or the baby.

Please try to understand and appreciate the corruptible seed and the "old man" that I used to be. Remember that ten seconds of rage I mentioned earlier when she confirmed that she was pregnant? My first thought was what size baseball bat I would use to bash his brains in. **"Repay no evil with evil" (Romans 12:17).** Over time, I found that the more I thought about Megan being pregnant, the more upset I became. And I knew that I needed prayer time and to surrender this to God.

My wife's mother came in for a visit to celebrate the twins' sixteenth birthday, and we decided not to tell her what was going on because of her age and several current health issues. While she was in town, I would drive and pick her up from church. One particular Sunday while waiting for her to come out, I began thinking about how close she must be with the Lord because she had recently told me that she had been attending church for over seventy years.

My sister-in-law Judy was told about the baby, and after the initial shock, she became a blessing to us by hiring a life coach for Megan. The pregnancy had created several long-term concerns, but it had also created a short-term problem namely, school.

Within several weeks, she began to show, and we did not want to send her to school pregnant. I thank God that virtual school had been established and was a very suitable option. With all of the bizarre behavior and security issues in the public school system, I had always been concerned about my child's safety.

Now I had the task of telling my older kids what was going on before they saw it on social media. My daughters were shocked but very understanding. Kevin was a different story. He was clearly angry because he had met the boyfriend before and looked at me and said, "What about other options? She is way too young to have a child." At least he got half of it right.

I calmly looked at him and said, "What if your mother and I had thought that about you?" If I had not been through the terrible experience with Grace forty years ago, we may have considered other options before he was born.

One of the blessings I looked forward to was that my two grandchildren would only be nine months apart. I purchased Megan a daily devotional and journal and asked her to read it every day and put her thoughts down on paper because this was a special time in her life, and she would cherish it in the years to come.

CHAPTER 10

A Joyful Heart Serves with Diligence

I stumbled across a Bible teacher who is the pastor at Park Side Church in Cleveland named Alistair Begg. His website is truthforlife. org, and the majority of his teachings are free to download. He has blessed me with his knowledge and compassion of the Bible.

He had done a series on the story of Joseph, the eleventh son born of Jacob. This series covered chapters 33 through 50 in the book of Genesis, and my first thoughts were that I really didn't remember the story of Joseph, just the multicolored coat. I was amazed how much print time he was given by God.

This series was twenty-four CDs, and he has the gift of storytelling in a practical spiritual way. I began burning hundreds of copies and giving them out because blessings should be extended to others (pay it forward).

March of 2012 was an unbelievable month for me. I had asked the youth minister at our church to allow me to give my personal testimony to her youth group. I barely knew this woman, and she may not have taken me seriously, but when I furnished her with a copy of my criminal charges and an outline of what I wanted to discuss, she agreed. Her group were thirteen- to fifteen-year-olds, and I had to tailor the message for their age group.

When I showed up, there were about 45–50 children, and I was very nervous but prayed that the Holy Spirit would use me as a vessel. I have always considered myself childlike and was very excited because these kids were educated and well versed.

When I started, I could hear my voice cracking and was sweating like I was at work. The Holy Spirit took over, and the next thing I remember was telling them thank you for the opportunity. I was later told that I spoke for over thirty minutes. Much to my surprise, they asked me a dozen questions when I finished, and one of them has stayed with me. The question proposed was quote three verses from memory and explain what they mean. How old were they? I responded with Romans 8:1, John 14:6, and John 15:5, which I believe to be the cornerstone of the gospel.

While working one morning, the local Christian radio station was giving away tickets to a Moody Men's Conference that was being held in Boca Raton. As I called the station, I prayed that if He wanted me to attend this conference, I would be the right caller. I won the tickets and gave the second ticket to my pastor who attended with one of the church elders and someone that I was in a growth group with.

What a blessing this was. The keynote speaker was Alistair Begg, and I was able to meet him and tell him how much I enjoyed his Bible teaching. The other speakers were Dr. Paul Nyquist, Walt McCord, and Haddon Robinson.

While I was there, I purchased several spiritual books, one of which was a book about the story of Daniel written by John Walvoord and revised and edited by Charles Dyer and Philip Rawley. I had recently been learning about scriptures that pertain to the end times, and when my pastor saw the book, he commented that he had done a paper for college on that exact book, and it was awesome but also said that the book of Daniel was one of the hardest reads in the Bible.

This book was basically a summary of the book of Daniel which included the actual verses with an explanation of scripture and what was going on in history at that point in time. It also discussed customs for those cultures and countries. The first six chapters were not too bad, but when I started the seventh, it became very difficult to understand.

It took me several weeks to finish the book, and when I was done, it had not resonated in my mind and heart. I thought about a second reread but decided to type a summary of the summary because as I said before, I retain much more of what I write.

When I was done with chapter 2, I realized that this information could be a blessing to others. It took me close to eight months to finish the writing, which was a hundred typed pages. I printed twenty-five copies and gave them out to my church family for Christmas gifts. Very few commented on the information, which concerned me because I knew that they had never even read it. Those that did were happy to have this information available to them.

I had now joined the outreach ministry called S & L Ministries which was started by Matthew and his wife Lisa. They were the ones who coordinated the Thanksgiving dinner, all of the brunches at the church, and also operated the church coffee shop. I had looked into numerous other outreach programs but had concerns about the way they were structured.

We met at the church and cooked the hot breakfast and headed to one of the downtown parks. A message was given before breakfast, and once again, I was amazed at how much they really listen and asked questions. The funny thing about doing community outreach is that you think that you are blessing those that are less fortunate, but in reality, you are being blessed for being the hands and feet of Christ. They have given me much more than I ever gave them.

A few weeks later, I began to think, *Why are we only doing this once a month?* One particular week on my day off, I went to KFC and purchased several buckets of chicken and had made up several bags of personal items. I showed up at the park unannounced, and they asked me why I had done this. I told them that God had blessed me and asked me to bless them through His provisions. They listened to a brief blessing, and we enjoyed some time together having lunch and talking.

While driving home, it dawned on me that with the money I had spent at KFC, I could have made a homemade feast for my friends at the park. A few weeks later, I made two sheet pans of lasagna, homemade meatballs, and a bucket of gravy and brought it to the park. I am fairly certain that they will never forget that lunch.

I had not seen Grace's mother at church and did not know if we were just attending different services or if her pain and guilt would not allow her to even see me anymore. Later that week, I felt led to call her so we could finally discuss our past.

Discussing this together seemed to bring both of us peace, and we ended our conversation knowing that Grace was in heaven and waiting to see us. I also told her what was going on with Megan, and she was happy that abortion was not a consideration. She also admitted that she had been avoiding seeing me at church. Thank You, Father, for your endless love and mercy.

On Good Friday, Kristy and Renee had agreed to attend the evening church service with me which made me excited, and she was bringing Kaylani, who was now five months old. I arrived early to visit the stages of the cross that my friend, the youth pastor, and her students had set up. I had never seen this in such detail, and what Jesus did for us really resonated with me. I felt blessed to be a child of God.

We attended the service, and Kristy did not feel comfortable putting Kaylani in the day care. Her decision to bring her into the church was the highlight of the evening. When the praise and worship began, my granddaughter began moving her hands and feet to the music, and I was told that she had never done that before. I gave her the nickname Gospel Girl.

When the service was over, we were talking in the parking area, and they said that they enjoyed the message. Kristy used to be an altar girl when she was younger at the church we were attending at the time. I began talking to them about accepting Christ but could tell that my words were falling on deaf ears, so I tried a different approach.

I told them the story of a British pastor who was asked to speak at the Moody church back in 1912 and had taken a ship from England to head to Chicago. The ship was the *Titanic*. He did not survive, but his last earthly words were trying to bring others to Christ. It had been one hundred years since the *Titanic* sank.

I tried using a parable about the *Titanic* and their salvation and my duties as a Christian and father. I told them that I was in one of the lifeboats in the water, and they were both still on the ship as it began to sink. I asked them to come into the boat which would save their lives, but they felt as though they could save themselves. I don't know if this resonated with them, but I tried planting a seed. As much as I laughed at my brother years ago, I do remember much of what he said.

Early Easter Sunday morning, we had breakfast at the beach, and I read verses from Matthew 28 and Romans 8 as we marveled at one of God's greatest creations. We attended our regular church as a family, and my oldest son, Kevin, met us there. I could not help but cry when I thought about what God had done in my life in just over one year.

I love the looks you get when a grown male cries and is not ashamed to give God the praise and glory. Kevin may have felt embarrassed, but he may remember that morning in the years to come after I am called home. Later that afternoon, we went up to Jupiter Beach for the church's baptism service. I always feel so blessed when I remember my own and love looking at their faces when they come up out of the water.

Later in the week, friends of mine from the growth group named Steve and Lisa called me and asked me to attend a function that they had scheduled. They are involved in an outreach ministry called Word in Deed Ministries that works with orphans in Uganda, West Africa. They are amazing people and have been a blessing to us.

As Katie and I got to know them better, we discovered that Lisa and Katie have the same birthday. From the first time I saw Steve, I recognized him and then realized that he was a pharmacist with a major retailer where I used to get my Rx. Weird, huh?

During the summer, I found out that the growth group leader, the youth group leader, and my friends from S & L Ministries were all leaving the church. I was told that there was not a conflict, but I could not help but think that people don't leave at the same time unless there is.

The church had a nice reception for the growth group leader because she had served for eighteen years, and that was the last time I saw her. As I investigated this, my conclusion was that they had a problem with the senior pastor and decided to move on.

One afternoon after work, I stopped by Kevin and Audrey's house unannounced. I had not seen them since the viewing of their grandson. I spent a few hours with them and told them my personal testimony and what God was doing in my life. Audrey was kind enough to share some stories about things that had happened in her life recently. I told them about the outreach breakfast at the park, and the following month, they attended and served with excellence.

In August, we planned a baby shower/party for Megan and invited about thirty-five family, friends, and neighbors. Our brothers and sisters blessed our daughter with much needed items and provisions for the baby.

As I suspected, the thought of adoption and/or giving up the baby was no longer being considered. Several people involved in the church asked us if we were interested in adoption because they knew wealthy couples that were looking to adopt an infant. My daughter chose God's gift over earthly treasures. Amen. Megan had decided to name the baby Juliette Rose.

My twins and I began having daily and/or weekly Bible studies whenever our schedules permitted. We concentrated on the Gospels, and I truly believe that they enjoyed learning about Christ and the Bible. The best compliment I could have ever received was from my son, who asked if he could read the scriptures during the Bible study. These meetings continued for several weeks.

I was discussing our Bible studies with one of the Tuesday night leaders, and he said something that I had never even considered. His comment was that "you are not only teaching your twins about the Lord, but Juliette could hear everything that was being said." This thought gave me such joy through the Lord.

The big day had finally arrived, and Katie and Megan were getting ready to head to the hospital. We prayed together, and she allowed me to bless her with anointed oil from Israel. They checked into the hospital birthing suite, and my daughter's doctor had discussed inducing labor because she had passed her due date.

Later that afternoon, I arrived at the hospital, and my daughter gave birth to my second granddaughter who weighed eight pounds and twelve ounces! Both were healthy and, once again, God blessed us with the miracle of childbirth.

A few weeks later, I woke up after having one of the most realistic and spirit-filled dreams that I have ever had. It was one of those rare dreams that you remember everything that happened, and I believe this to be the answer to my earlier prayer.

It began with me flying over the beach at the area I discussed earlier coined double roads. It looked the way it did forty years ago, and I was flying without any man-made devices. I continued flying further out into the ocean and noticed four docks in the middle of nowhere. The first one had an enormous cruise ship. The second dock had a large fifty-foot cigarette boat. The third dock had a Jet Ski, and the fourth had a small two-person paddleboat. As I looked at the docks, I began thinking that the cruise ship was for those who wanted to be served. The cigarette boat was for those who wanted extreme and rapid pleasure. The Jet Ski was for those who wanted recreational pleasure, and the paddleboat was for those who relied on their own ability. The next moment, I was inside the cruise ship standing with Grace's mother and several people I knew from high school. I was serving them food and told Grace's mother that I enjoyed serving others, and she deserved to be served. I did not think that the last part of the dream was odd until the following morning when I checked Facebook. The majority of the people from my dream had gotten together at a local restaurant and were standing there with plates of food in their hands!

My thoughts regarding this dream were extremely confusing. Was God trying to tell me to serve with a loving heart or make a decision on what I wanted? I continued thinking and praying about this dream and its meaning.

I had heard on the radio that October was pastor appreciation month. Wow, who knew. I wanted to do something for our pastors, and we usually rely on what we know. In my case, it is cooking and serving food. I called one of the pastors and asked him if I could bring in lunch for the church staff, and after checking with the others, we set up a luncheon for later in the week.

I guess that they thought I was bringing sandwiches or something from a local restaurant. I had learned from my studies that anything you do for the glory of God should be done in excellence. I cooked an entire sheet pan of lasagna, a dozen meatballs and sausage in a gallon of gravy, two loaves of garlic bread, and a key lime pie. I can still see their faces when I wheeled the food into their conference room, and the smell filled the room. Our senior pastor commented on the food for the next several weeks. Thanks, Mom.

Thanksgiving was approaching, and after a few meetings with S & L Ministries, we decided to raise funds and help underprivileged families for the upcoming holiday We packaged up three dozens complete dinners and passed them out to several families and also several established church outreach programs. All food and other items were either donated by local restaurants or from funds collected.

November was the first time I was asked to give the monthly message at the park for our brothers and sisters, which this time of year is usually about 60–70 people. God put it on my heart to talk about my past and my personal testimony, and once again, I was brutally honest and transparent to a fault.

I was very nervous when I started, but the Holy Spirit took over, and I was told that it was an inspiring message. I am still amazed how acceptable they are to the message compared to "regular" people. I tried to talk to them as friends and show them respect.

Remember when I said I have a heart for the needy and homeless? Well, Christmas was a few weeks away, and I had always thought how difficult it would be to live on the streets, especially on Christmas morning. I discussed this with the Tuesday night Bible study group and also several other people in my biblical circles. We talked about what we could do for our brothers and sisters on Jesus's birthday.

We collected funds and thought that new backpacks, clothes, and personal hygiene items would be a blessing. We spent the next few weeks visiting secondhand stores and managed to purchase forty-five backpacks and filled them with the much needed items. We had also planned on serving a hot breakfast.

On Christmas morning, several of us went down to the park very early, and they were extremely excited and surprised that someone was there for them on Jesus's birthday. We spent about an hour with them eating breakfast, passing out the gifts, and giving them a short message about God and His awesome grace and mercy.

Johnny and Megan went with me, and we felt so blessed to be a part of Jesus's hands and feet. I can honestly say that there is no better feeling than when we allow God to work through us. **"Now if anyone builds on this foundation, with gold, silver, precious stones, wood, hay, straw, each one's work will become manifest; for the Day will declare it, because it will be revealed by fire; and the fire will test each one's work, of what sort it is" (1 Corinthians 3:12–13).**

I find this hard to put into words, but I will do my best. Talking about Christ to people who have no earthly possessions or apparent hope seems to be the hardest message there is. I have never been able to put into words how special they are because if they could preach the Gospel with abundant joy, I think it would really resonate with people, compared to a healthy/wealthy pastor. **"Blessed are the meek, for they shall inherit the earth" (Matthew 5:5).**

CHAPTER 11

You Reap What You Sow

I was contacted by my friends at S & L Ministries and asked to give the message for the January meeting at the park. My mother-in-law and sister-in-law, Patty, were visiting and decided to attend with us. I was very excited and began thinking about what message the Lord might give me. I was honored and also very nervous when I began talking, and once again, the Holy Spirit took over. We talked about the difference between the Old and New Testament (the law versus grace), and they seemed to receive the message I had intended. If you have never attended an outreach function, I suggest you try the experience. My only advise would be to start small because it can become overwhelming very quickly.

Toward the end of February, our landlord told me that she wanted to sell the house and put it on the market by April. After several meetings with her, I was able to convince her to allow us to remain in the property till the end of the year.

Over the next few months, I think the Holy Spirit was trying to give me a message because He knew what was ahead, but as I said before, the busyness of life blinds us. I began packing up what I could and continued looking at possible rentals but did not find anything that we liked or could afford.

In May, my boss asked me to return to the Tampa office and conduct a two-day training class for their existing and new investigators. I have always enjoyed training investigators. I drove over early in the morning. It was my birthday. I had made arrangements to spend the evening with my dear friends who lived nearby.

I have known Robin since I was five years old, and she grew up a few houses from mine in the old neighborhood. I had met Jimmy in high school, and they started dating when they were about fifteen and have now been married over thirty years. After work, I met them at their house, and we had dinner together at one of my favorite restaurants.

We spent the rest of the evening talking about the past and what God had done in our lives. Robin and Jimmy had accepted Christ at a young age and matured like most people should. I have enormous love and respect for them because they had put five children through college and had always put their children first and their comfort and personal goals second. They are one of the few couples that I know that have actually allowed God to control their lives.

I talked with them about the problems that I was having back home regarding my relationships with the older children because of things that I did and failed to do. Jimmy said something that was so simple but would change my relationship with them. He asked me if I had ever told them that I was sorry. His statement blew me away because I realized I had not. Repentance and prayer have always worked for me in the past. Sometimes we take things for granted and just assume that others know how we feel and what we are thinking.

I returned home and had a nice birthday celebration with my family, even though the older kids were unavailable. During the next several weeks, I met with all five of my children separately and told them that I was sorry for my behavior while they were growing up and asked for their forgiveness. Once again, I realized that we have to take a step of faith outside of our comfort zone and humble ourselves before others.

The following month, my friends from S & L Ministries called us to let us know that they were going to attend a fundraiser at a local restaurant for one of their employees who had cancer and was currently in treatment. She is a single mother, and her health insurance had a huge deductible. We did not have much money but planned on attending.

We enjoyed the fellowship with our friends, and I wished that we could have done more to help this young lady. The fruit of the

Spirit was flowing as numerous people in attendance donated awesome items for the silent auction.

I truly enjoy this type of function because this fruit is seen and felt immediately. As I stated before, I wish we could have done more, but my monthly wages were down 40–50 percent because of my employer not having enough work. **"Seek first the kingdom of God, and all these things will be given to you" (Matthew 6:33).**

I only mention the above financial concerns to remind us how awesome God is, and He knows our smallest worries and problems. The following weekend, I attended the monthly meeting for S & L, which we usually had before the outreach breakfast for our brothers and sisters. When I was leaving the meeting, Matthew handed me a card, and I thought it might be a thank-you card for volunteering my time.

When I got home, Katie asked me what the card was for, and I told her it must be a thank-you card. She said, "Why don't you open it?"

When I did, I was speechless. There was a check from the ministry for five hundred dollars, the exact amount that I was short for the upcoming rent. When I asked them why they had given it to me, they told me that God put it on their hearts to help us with expenses for the baby. God is good!

I don't know if it was the stress of the large rent payment, my concerns for my children and grandchildren, knowing that my wife and I now only talk about problems, and there is no joy, where we were going to move, where would we get the money to move, or working a job that I hated, but I found myself starting to drink and smoke again. **"And do not be drunk with wine, in which is dissipation; but be filled with the Spirit" (Ephesians 5:18).**

It pains me just to write that because I know better, and I have received more grace and mercy than three lifetimes. God is enough; my spirit cries, but my flesh and mind are battling the spirit. I was not drinking as much as I used to, but I was still being influenced by the flesh.

In July, we were receiving heat from our families about having Juliette baptized. I will try not to spend much time on this subject because, quite honestly, everyone has a different belief, depending on what you were taught and believe. Personally, I was taught to have a child baptized within a month of being born so they would have God's blessing and receive the benefits of baptism. What about the age of accountability? What about the original sin? Were we baptizing the flesh or the spirit or both? As we began to really think about this, we decided that a christening and/or dedication might be a good idea.

During the next few days, I tried praying and meditating about children who die young and their final destination regarding eternity. I have often had lengthy conversations with close friends about this topic. I am unaware of any verses that define God's plan for this event. My sister-in-law, Cheryl, who has forgotten more about the Bible than I will ever know was only able to find one verse that is even close. **"Can I bring him back again? I shall go to him, but he shall not return to me" (2 Samuel 12:23).** This verse was in reference to King David after he lost his firstborn with Bathsheba after the Prophet Nathan visited him.

"The gang" attended the christening, and my friend from the Tuesday night Bible study said he would lead the prayer and also the christening which would be done in our swimming pool. This was truly a gift from heaven and one of His precious blessings. Even some of our family members who regularly attend one of the legalistic churches seemed to love this unique and holy moment.

Johnny filmed the event, and when I watch the video, it is truly precious. I was in the swimming pool holding Juliette as the pastor prayed and told us that we were dedicating this child back to God. As he spoke, I could feel a tingling in my arms and a positive energy being transferred from the pastor to my granddaughter and to me. This feeling was very similar to the feeling when I received the physical healing.

At the end of the summer, we celebrated Juliette's first birthday, and I tried to give God the praise and glory. Prior to serving the food, all of us held hands in a circle and thanked God for our granddaughter and His daily blessings. Juliette and Megan received many beautiful gifts and also some much needed funds. We did not receive any calls or gifts from my daughter's ex-boyfriend or his family, and they have been silent lately. The following year, we heard they had moved to North Florida.

I had been looking but still had not found a new place to move into, and we were unable to put away any money. Something that continued to bother me was that my wife seemed to not want to be around me. She had prayed for me for over fifteen years to be the man that she wanted, and now she seemed to care less. Trust me, I understand that I put this woman through hell, but if she wanted a divorce, she would just say so.

I continued packing up what I could in the house, and Megan also started packing up her stuff and the baby's stuff. It was getting closer to the end of October and I came home one afternoon, and all of my religious and spiritual books, journals, handwritten ledgers, DVDs, CDs, Bibles, and contact information had been packed up by my wife. At first I was happy to see that she had started packing things up, until I realized that she had not packed up any of her stuff, just mine.

I wish I could tell you that I was a loving husband and caring Christian, but the complete opposite was true. **"Keep your heart with all diligence, for out of it springs the issues of life" (Proverbs 4:23).** We had a huge fight, and once again, I allowed her to steal my peace and joy. I know some of you may be thinking that if I really had Christ's peace and joy that no other person should be able to steal it.

My wife and I still love each other, but I am not sure that we truly like each other. We ignored each other for a few days, and on my next day off, I began packing up some old VHS tapes, and when I walked out of the room, she removed half of the tapes from the box. When I asked "what are you doing?" Katie told me that she wanted to separate and get her own place with the kids.

We have been together for over twenty-one years, and it is always difficult when you realize that you have not been the man that you promised to be. Even though it sounds terrible to say, my only thought was that I would no longer be living with the kids.

I later asked Johnny and Megan if they wanted to live with me, and after they stopped laughing, they said no. I know I deserve everything that was happening, but it still broke my heart. But I refused to allow Satan to continue to deceive me.

During the next few weeks, Megan and I packed up the entire house and had all of the boxes in the garage ready to be transported. She told me that Katie had found a nice rental in the area. We had been discussing who was taking what, and I did not want to argue about materialistic possessions. I suggested that she take everything except my personal belongings, which was definitely God working through me because I used to worry about such insignificant matters.

I had been so busy and concerned with the move that it had not dawned on me that I was about to be homeless. **"I have learned to be content in any situation or surrounding" (Philippians 4:12).** I contacted the landlord and advised her of what was going on and that we might need another two weeks in the property, which was the money I had saved to get a place. Being a caring Christian woman, she told me that we could stay at the house until we were ready to move.

On Saturday, November 16, Megan and I moved everything to their new place while Katie and Johnny both worked all day. Surprisingly, I was happy for them and truly believe that my wife deserves a fresh start, and she was excited about having her own place again. I know that this sounds bizarre to those of you that have a caring and loving marriage, but if you have paid attention to our lives, we lost our closeness and deep love many years ago.

I recontacted the landlord and told her that my wife and kids were moved out, and she asked me where I was going because she knew that I did not have anywhere to go. She told me I could stay at the house for a few more weeks at no cost to me if I was willing to help out with the renovations, but the house would need to be empty of all furniture and personal belongings.

When I returned to the empty lonely house that evening, reality set in, and I cried like a baby and thanked God for still loving and protecting me. I did not have a pity party or purchase bug bombs, which I contribute to God and His amazing grace.

I stayed away from my wife's new place for a few weeks even though it broke my heart not seeing my children and especially Juliette. We were short of our twentieth anniversary by eleven days. I was so thankful for what God had done in my life during the last few years because I no longer sat around feeling sorry for myself. I began to realize that even though my life was about to change again, I currently had a roof over my head, indoor plumbing, hot and cold water, food in the house, a propane grill, and money in my pocket.

Through my landlord's caring spirit and God's never-ending grace, I was able to remain at the property for thirty days. Due to the money I was spending on some of the property's repairs, the monies owed for our rental's utilities and a costly car repair, I was unable to save enough money to find a new place.

It was getting close to Christmas, and my friends and I began to discuss what we were going to do for our brothers and sisters whom we delivered the backpacks to last year. We had asked several people for donations, but it appeared the economy is especially tight this year.

We decided to pass out brand-new sleeping bags, clothes, and personal hygiene items. We found forty-five brand-new sleeping bags for about five hundred dollars. Thank you, overstock.com. The true peace, joy, and happiness that God gives you from doing something nice for others without strings is one of His greatest blessings.

I had sent out Christmas cards the first week of December and sent cards to everyone in my wife's family, which may have shocked them. I heard from my friends Kevin and Audrey, and they thanked me for the Christmas card. A few days later, we got together for lunch, and it was so nice spending time with them in a joyful setting and not at a funeral.

They honestly seemed concerned when I told them that I did not know where I was going after I leave the rental property. They told me to call them after the New Year if I needed a place to stay but had their daughter and grandchildren in town for the holidays.

My friends have been drawn closer to God after the death of their grandson. I certainly am not smart enough to understand how

He uses death as a vessel to Himself but will know all things when I have the mind of Christ.

On Tuesday, December 17, 2013, I had to leave the property and loaded my car with the few personal items. I remember that feeling when I drove out of the subdivision and this 300K house. Where am I going? I was officially homeless. Several of my friends had offered to let me stay at their homes but were unavailable when I had called.

I spent a week living in my car, which certainly is an adjustment. The hardest part of living in your car is where to go to the bathroom and take a shower. Using grocery stores, hotels, and restaurants to use the restroom and showering at the beach at night certainly puts your life in perspective.

Although my current living situation was difficult on my flesh and mind, I had not felt as close to God for several years. I realized that when we have nothing left but God, God is enough. When all of our daily distractions are removed, we are able to really appreciate Him and His awesome love and wisdom that He provides for us. Kind of like the story of Job, with the exception that I am not as obedient, holy, or righteous.

A few days before Christmas, my sister and brother-in-law, Judy and Michael, had invited us up to Vero Beach for a Christmas dinner and fellowship. Katie and Johnny had to work so Megan, Juliette, and I went. After dinner, I went outside to have a smoke and was thinking about telling them about my current living situation, but I felt a little awkward being there, now that Katie and I had separated.

Within five minutes, Judy asked me where I was staying, and I was being somewhat evasive. She asked me if I was living in my car. I did not want to lie to her, so I said yes, but it was fine. When we were leaving, they handed me a roll of cash and told me to get a place, but I did not have peace about accepting their generous gift.

I know that they may have been trying to help me, but I have been bailed out my entire life by other people and as I told them, there are actions and reactions in this life and also consequences for these actions. I felt as though it was time for me to grow up, and being without a home or the modern conveniences in life is not the worst thing that I could imagine; being without Christ is.

The following afternoon, my son Kevin told me that he was going to take the holiday baton and have a Christmas Eve party at his house. I was so happy that our holiday party would not end just because of my current living situation.

Kevin offered to let me stay the night, and when my wife and twins left later that evening, I realized that this would be the first Christmas morning that I would not celebrate with family doing the present thing.

At first light, I visited the park for my brothers and sisters for our Christmas morning celebration. Once again, they were so joyful and grateful that someone would care about them on Jesus's birthday. A few hours of our time meant the world to those less fortunate than most. Even though my life was in turmoil, I had much more than most of them and once again thanked God for his love, grace, and mercy. I remember thinking, *What are we going to buy for them the following Christmas?*

Katie had invited me over for Christmas dinner when we were at Kevin's, and I felt so blessed to spend Christmas afternoon with them, even though she forgot to buy anything for dinner. Thank the Lord for Domino's. Anyway, I ended up spending the night there and sleeping on the floor, which never felt so good after being in the car.

The following evening, I was back in the car but spent several hours walking on the beach and remembered something that I had either read or heard. The ocean is like God; no matter how hard you try to see and appreciate it all, He only allows you to see and appreciate what you are able to understand. **"I still have many things to say to you, but you cannot bear them now" (John 16:12).**

A few days after Christmas, I woke up and had a bad stomach pain but thought that I just needed to use the bathroom. Throughout the day, the pain increased, and later that evening, I called Kevin and asked if I could stay at his house again. He agreed.

When I woke up the following morning, the pain had increased, and I knew something was wrong. I spent the majority of the day just praying and trying to get through the day. Later that evening,

I stopped at a store to use the restroom and noticed that there was blood. It takes a lot for me to go to the doctor, but I knew something serious was going on.

I went to the emergency room and was told that I had a serious case of diverticulitis, which is an infection and inflammation of the colon. They admitted me and began pumping me with antibiotics and pain medication. I remember laughing when I wondered if this was God's way of getting me out of the car.

After four days of lying in a hospital bed, I started walking through the halls, pushing my IV pole. Within a few minutes, I saw someone that I was sure that I knew. She was a girl that I grew up with from the old neighborhood, but she looked like she was 10–15 years older than me, even though I knew she was my age. I went back to my room and ignored my first instinct, convincing myself that it must not have been her.

The next day, I saw her again and was certain it was her. I went into her room, and she did not recognize me. She did not look well. I told her who I was, and she smiled and said it was great to see me. I told her why I was in the hospital, and she told me that she was there for a blood transfusion, which concerned me. I know that there are only a few reasons why you have a blood transfusion, and none of them are good.

We talked for several minutes, and I could not get over how old she looked. Trying not to judge, I just smiled, and we continued talking about grade school through high school and the last time we saw each other. Her nurse came in, and we said goodbye. I told her I would stop by later or the next day.

I returned to my room, and several minutes later, the Holy Spirit told me to return to her room and give her my personal testimony and what He had done for me over the last few years. I usually am somewhat obedient to the voice of God, but I had a problem with what I was being instructed to do. **"There is none righteous, no, not one." (Romans 3:10).**

The reason was that the last time I saw her was in January 1982 when I lived in Colorado and flew home for Christmas. We had seen each other at the neighborhood bar, and after last call, we sat in her car for several hours doing cocaine. She wanted to get intimate, but consuming that much cocaine can create problems. She had called me when I returned to Colorado and asked me why I would not have sex with her. I explained why and told her that I was always attracted to her when we were growing up.

Anyway, my point here is that my flesh and mind were telling me that I would sound like a hypocrite now that I was peddling the Good News. My flesh and spirit battled back and forth for the rest of the day, and I allowed my flesh to convince myself that I would pray on it and go and see her the next day. Pray on it? I had just received a command from God Almighty and ignored Him.

The next morning, I went to her room and saw that it was empty. I asked her nurse where she was, and she told me that she had been discharged. I went back to my room and felt so convicted that I had ignored the Holy Spirit. I knew her mother still lived in the old neighborhood and told myself that I would visit her after I got out of the hospital.

I remained at the hospital for another week, and my children and wife visited me, which made me feel good, even though I did spend New Year's Eve alone. It reminded me how far God had brought me since that New Year's Eve in the hotel room only three years ago. It amazed me how much God had changed my heart and my attitude.

During the last six weeks, my wife of twenty years left me, my children laughed when I asked them to live with me, I was separated from Juliette for the first time, my dog of ten years died, I was broke and homeless but had Christ, and that was all that really mattered.

Shortly after being released from the hospital, I heard from Robin, my friend from Tampa. She had called to ask me if I had heard that the woman from the hospital had just died!! I was devastated. She told me that she had suffered from various substance abuse problems and had been in and out of treatment centers for several years.

My next thought was that I may have been the last person on this planet to help bring her to the Lord, and I didn't do it because of my foolish ego and pride. When the Holy Spirit gives you the urge, please listen to Him. **"And do not grieve the Holy Spirit of God,**

by whom you were sealed for the day of redemption" (Ephesians 4:30).

Katie called me right after New Year's and said that she wanted me to stay with them after I got released from the hospital because she knew that I had no place to live. Through God's love, she had extended the olive branch, and I spent a week with them sleeping on the couch. I missed another two weeks of work as I tried to recuperate.

Kevin and Audrey called me to tell me that their family members were returning home and asked me to stay with them. I felt awkward at first because as I said before, I had only seen them a few times during the last several decades, but I believe that friendships that started during adolescence pass the test of time. I was excited when they told me that they attended the church where I was baptized a few years earlier.

My plan was to stay with them until I could save enough money to get my own place. After a few weeks with my friends, I began to realize that the hundreds of pictures of their grandson were a huge part of their grieving process.

They attend church and visit the grave site regularly, but their joy had been stolen. It had been less than three years. I had asked them several times to attend and/or have a Bible study, but all I could do at this point was to plant the seed.

CHAPTER 12

Peace and Joy during Trials and Tribulation

I have never been one for new year's resolutions but found myself thinking more and more about the older kids and how to be a better parent to them. I realized that the only time I really see them is on holidays, birthdays, and special occasions. I decided to try and be a bigger part of their lives.

By the end of January, Kristy and Renee both told me that they were pregnant, and Kristy was having a boy. Her due date would be around the second week of August, a week after her birthday. Renee and Ian were so excited to be having their first child together. Ian has a twelve-year-old son named Ethan from a prior marriage, and Renee is an awesome stepmother. Her due date was the beginning of September.

I had been talking with Kevin, and he told me that he and his girlfriend, Jodi, were planning a vacation to Asheville, North Carolina, and he had planned on proposing to her. They were gone about a week and I was happy to hear that everything went well and she said yes. They had tentatively set the date for March 2015 and were planning a destination wedding in Charleston, South Carolina.

Katie continued working two jobs, and I usually picked up Megan and Juliette on Mondays and took them to lunch. Johnny was seldom around due to school and working, but I usually saw him on the weekends when I visited.

I had returned to work, and my health continued to improve, but my employer never seemed to have enough work, and I began to sense that the new office manager was trying to starve me out of a job. My ex-partner was approaching retirement and seldom around.

My prayer life improved and there were times when the glory and presence of the Lord was thick and I felt that feeling that I have only felt a few times in my life. My take on this is that this is His way of telling us that we are never alone.

One of my friends from Bible study told me about a pastor she knew that had the anointed gift of healing and had a ministry that met on Sunday evenings. I considered calling my friend from North Carolina but decided to try a healing in person because my stomach/colon issues were not improving.

We visited the church, and much to my surprise, he was in his eighties, and most of the congregation were also elderly. He took me into a room before the service began, and I started talking with two of his associate pastors. I thought I was there for a physical healing, but my health issues never came up.

They asked me to briefly describe myself and my life, and when I told them that my wife and I were currently separated, that seemed to spark their interest. They asked me, if they were to ask my wife why, what her answer would be. I told them that primarily because of my substance abuse, selfishness, and infidelity.

When they found out that I had been married twice before and had also committed adultery in the prior marriages, they had me repeat after them while they prayed an extremely long prayer asking for a spiritual healing. As I spoke these words, I began to feel a calming and peaceful feeling and thanked God when they finished.

They began to talk about something called soul ties, and as they continued, they began to freak me out. They were telling me that while I was involved in the physical act of sex, while committing adultery, it was more than just the physical act. They stated that my spirit was connecting with their spirit and every spirit that they had ever slept with, hence the term *soul ties*.

They suggested that I repent in private to God for these physical acts of adultery and to also write down every name of the women

114

I slept with, and the senior pastor would also pray to God on my behalf. When one of them returned with a pencil and an index card, I could not help but laugh and told them I would need more paper.

They asked me to give them a rough estimate of how many people I had slept with, and when I did, they stared at me like I was Charles Manson. I told them that this was not something that I was prepared to do today but would write down all of the names and return next Sunday.

We attended the service, and a healing prayer was given to me and many others when they had the altar call. I think all spiritual healing is unique and different for different people. I have seen people healed immediately but have never experienced this myself. The important thing to me was that I was among children of God, in a holy setting, and the glory of God was present.

During the next several days, I began seriously thinking about the names and events of the last thirty-plus years and had to ask the Holy Spirit for assistance and guidance because half of the names were while I was in a drunken stupor or whacked out on narcotics or both. I have always been amazed how the Holy Spirit works if we are sincere, faith filled, and able to receive our requests. The amount of thoughts and memories I received from the past still amazes me.

I returned the following Sunday with my scroll and gave it to the associate pastors, and once again, they had me repeat after them as they said a lengthy prayer. I attended the service again, and I was amazed at how loving and caring this group was. During the next few days, I began feeling better and having less stomach irritation. Kevin and Audrey attended with me.

In early February, we celebrated our twins' eighteenth birthday, and I took them out for a nice dinner, and of course, Katie had to work. When I returned to Kevin and Audrey's that evening, I began thinking about all of the events of their lives and all of the good times we had while they were small children. I also could not help but think about all of the times that I had disappointed them, and it amazes me how we remember the bad times easier than the good.

I had been listening to my favorite Christian radio station that was having a pledge drive to sponsor children in developing countries. I visited their website and was amazed that there were thousands of children in dozens of countries waiting to be sponsored. I decided to sponsor two children from Togo, Africa, and requested that they use my monthly donations to choose two children that have been waiting the longest to be sponsored.

Their names are Mickel and Nazif. They are five and eight years old, and as I read about their village and their lifestyle, I could not help but realize how blessed I am. One of them does not have a father, and both of their families only earn about one dollar a day. That amount is hard to comprehend, and when I realized that I spend more on cigarettes in a month than they earn in half a year, I realized how disobedient and selfish I am. Their birthdays were in February and March, and I sent them each fifty-five dollars to celebrate and to also help out with their daily struggles.

The Compassion International website is user friendly, and they provide templates that you can use to write letters to the children. I have written them several letters each and have also received three letters from each of them. When I was informed that only the children who are sponsored attend school, I felt so good about what I had decided to do.

The funny thing about being a sponsor is that you feel so blessed when you realize that you are changing someone's life for less than a cup of coffee per day. The truth of the matter is that I receive more joy from their letters than most anything else in life.

A few days after Valentine's Day, Kristy told me that Renee had lost the baby recently, and it actually happened on Valentine's Day. I felt so bad for her and Ian. I sent her a text and told her that I loved her and to call me if she needed anything. I decided to write her a letter and tried to give her words of encouragement and love and why bad things happen in this sin-filled world. I tried to quote her scripture that might put her heart at ease, but time and prayer are usually the best medicine. I closed the letter by telling her about Grace and what happened when I was a teenager and that her child was in heaven waiting to see her. She called me after receiving the letter and thanked me for taking the time to write it and to also send it through snail mail.

Later that day, I received a call from my godmother, Vivian, who told me that our first cousin Tommy was currently in hospice and may not live much longer. He was a huge part of my childhood and was my favorite cousin, even though he was about fifteen years older than me.

I had only seen him a few times in the last twenty to twenty-five years because we had lost contact after we had gotten older and after our parents passed. When I walked into his room, I did not even recognize him. He was not coherent, but the nursing staff told us that he could probably hear us. We visited about an hour and then left, but I could not help but wonder where his wife was.

I returned to the hospital the following day, and there were no visitors—no cards, no flowers, and no evidence of being a husband, a friend, a family member, or a human being. I could not help but think about how many thousands of people we meet and come across in our lifetime and how there are very few of them at the end of this carnal life. **"I will never leave or forsake you" (Joshua 1:5, Hebrews 13:5).**

I visited the hospital gift shop and bought a vase with three colored roses and a small card. I cut two of the stems and arranged them to imitate the three crosses and wrote "Come home, I am waiting" and signed the card "Jesus." I took his hand and spoke to him from my heart and was inspired by the Holy Spirit when I told him that I loved him and thanked him for all of the things that he did for me when I was a kid. I also told him that he was dying and if he did not have a personal relationship with Jesus, now was the time. I asked him to accept Jesus as his personal Savior and repent for all of his earthly sins. I closed with telling him that I would see him when Jesus calls me home.

I left the hospital and continued thinking and praying for him. I found myself not asking for him to be healed but to be called home. He was called home the following day after a local priest had visited him that morning to minister to him. Vivian told me that a celebration was being planned for him within a few weeks.

My mother-in-law and Patty who had visited the prior year came in for the afternoon because they had been visiting Judy in Vero

Beach. Katie was at work, and I just happened to be visiting when they arrived. They had not seen the baby since she was five months old, and I decided to take them out to dinner. The six of us went to a nice restaurant.

It was nice spending time with them, but as we were finishing, they began speaking a spirit of legalistic nonsense. They began telling Megan that her child was a mistake and that God was not pleased with her. They then told me that my oldest daughter was living in sin because she had a child and was expecting another and was not married. **"Death and life are in the power of the tongue, and those who love it will eat its fruit" (Proverbs 18:21).**

Megan and Johnny were visibly upset and took the baby and left the restaurant and waited outside. I am like most parents in the sense that it does not bother me when you attack me, but when you attack my children…

I found myself battling the flesh and asking the Holy Spirit to give me His love, patience, and wisdom because if I said what was on my mind, I would not be a good witness for Christ. Through His wisdom, I told them that if they were looking to blame someone, they needed to blame me because I was never the spiritual head of the family and did not raise them with biblical truths and/or in a godly environment.

I calmly told them that I was not crazy about the things that were going on, but giving *all* of your cares and concerns to God was the only thing that mattered. I tried to explain to them that my daughters' lives and actions were really none of our business, and if they believed in faith, they would just pray for God's protection and blessings.

I was actually proud of myself because I was defeating the flesh with His words with/in/through me. I was extending grace and feel spiritually sorry for those who still live by the letter of the law. **"But now we have been delivered from the law, having died to what we were held by, so that we should serve in the newness of the Spirit and not in the oldness of the letter" (Romans 7:6).** I had been praying to Him to help me receive His love and wisdom in times of emotional turmoil.

We left the restaurant. My children had cooled down, and we went back to the house. I spoke with my mother-in-law and Patty and assured me that their only concern are for my daughters and granddaughters. We prayed together before they headed back to Vero.

April 20 was Easter Sunday, and I attended church with Kevin and Audrey. They didn't appreciate my humor when I pointed out that the date was the national day for marijuana usage. I was blessed to have Easter dinner with my entire family at Kristy's house and truly enjoyed seeing everyone.

The following Sunday was the outreach breakfast that S & L Ministries puts on each month, and I was so happy to see this woman that I had met the prior year at one of our meetings. The first time I met her, she opened the meeting in prayer, and I was blown away. She opened her prayer by thanking God for waking her up this morning and said that there must be something that you want me to do today because you woke me up! I had never even thought about that statement.

As I began talking with her, she told me that she had recently retired after being a DCF investigator for close to thirty years and is involved in several outreaches and underprivileged organizations. I noticed that she was now using a walker as she made her way through the grass to the picnic tables. I hugged her, and she told me that she had been thinking about me lately and was giving the message today before we served God's provisions.

When she started her message, she once again opened her prayer for thanking God for waking her up this morning, and I could not help but get emotional when she said that she had recently developed gangrene and had to have several of her toes amputated, but the blessing was that they were able to save her foot. She also stated that she thought it was God's way of telling her to slow down and stop trying to save the world. I spoke with her for several minutes after the breakfast, until she said that she had to leave and return home and get ready for church.

I could not stop thinking about her, and a few days later, God put it on my heart to do something for her and her husband. I cooked two dozen manicotti and a few pounds of sausage, along with the gravy and garlic bread, and told her that I wanted to bless her because she has blessed so many.

I dropped off the blessing and got to meet with them and gave her a copy of this manuscript. She laid hands on me and prayed over me before I left, and I truly felt our spirits joyfully mingling.

Later that week, Katie and I received our federal tax refund, and I told her to just keep the check and credit my share toward the money that I give her each month for my health and auto insurance. She reminded me that I needed to endorse the check and said that she would call me later in the week so we could get together.

Within a few days, Katie stopped by so I could endorse the check, and she suggested that I just go to the bank with her so we could cash the check. We were standing in line, and one of the tellers kept looking at me like she knew me, which normally would not be a concern, but we were in a bank.

She called our number and continued giving me a hard look and asked me where I got my hat which says "John 15:5" on the front. I told her that a friend of mine made it for me along with two others. She said that she had recently attended her first Bible study where they spent several hours talking about that verse. She was spirit filled and said that God brought me to her line, which I agree with because there were numerous tellers.

We were walking to the car, and Katie asked me if this happened frequently, and I told her not as often as I had hoped. Moments later, she put her arm around me and her head on my shoulder and told me how much she loved me and thanked me for allowing God into my life. That was a very special moment for me because we showed physical love toward each other.

When she dropped me off, she gave me a Benjamin and squeezed me so hard I could barely breathe. I know that God can repair any relationship, but I was amazed at the feelings that she showed toward me and had given me hope in our marriage.

CHAPTER 13

Romans 7:14-17

For we know that the law is spiritual, but I am carnal, sold under sin. For what I am doing, I do not understand. For what I will to do, that I do not practice; but what I hate, that I do. If then, I do what I will not to do, I agree with the law that it is good. But now, it is no longer I who do it, but sin that dwells in me.
—Romans 7:14–17

It was now the middle of May and my birthday. I am not one of those people that others make a fuss over when it is their birthday. Honestly, I am happy if I receive a few texts and emails. Anyway, most of my family was working or just busy with life, and I was feeling a little down. I went to the restaurant where PJ worked and had planned on having dinner, which never happened.

The restaurant was packed, and I found an empty stool at the bar and had a few Grand Mariners. A friend of mine met me there, and after a few hours, the three of us went to a local watering hole. It turned out that my friend's sons were friends with PJ. Well, the two of them were talking, and I was just trying to act like I was interested.

An attractive woman in her early forties sat down next to me, and we began talking. I could tell that she had also been drinking, and after a few minutes, she told me that today was her birthday. Being suspicious of that statement, she had to show me her driver's license before I believed her.

During our second drink, she looked at me and asked me if I wanted to go to the beach and hang out. I just looked at her and said, "What? I don't even know you."

I told her that I was married, and she said "so am I," and the thing that we have in common is that we are both married to women. She also said that she was recently separated and told me that I looked harmless, a little lonely, and was somehow drawn to me. I was shocked to say the least.

Considering that being intimate was off the table, I became intrigued by her proposal. The thought of witnessing to her because she was gay suddenly fired me up. I have never really tried talking with someone who was gay about the Lord, even though I had thought about it in the past. **"There is therefore now no condemnation to those who are in Christ Jesus, who do not walk according to the flesh, but according to the Spirit" (Romans 8:1).**

I said goodbye to my friends and rode with her to the beach, and we sat and talked for about an hour about God, her faith, and beliefs. She told me that she believed in God but did not go to church because she knew how He felt about being gay. I began thinking how awesome it was that she said that, but I also know what the Word says, and most of it is about love, hope, and faith.

I told her that God loved her very much, regardless of her sexual preference, her past, or her lifestyle. **"As far as the east is from the west, so far as He removed our transgressions from us" (Psalm 103:12).** I listened as she talked about her life and why she was no longer living with her partner. As she continued sharing, I could not help but think that their relationship was no different from a typical marriage. She had the same problems, the same concerns, and just wanted to feel loved like the rest of us.

I also was transparent and told her about why I was separated from Katie and living at Kevin and Audrey's and how much I missed my kids and not seeing the grandchildren as much as I would have liked. I gave her a *Reader's Digest* version of my carnal life and how and when I accepted Jesus. I also asked her to attend church with me and let her know that several gays attended on a regular basis. She said that she had not been to a church in over a decade and would have to think about it.

Remember how alcohol helps you make bad decisions? Well, I got the bright idea to go swimming. There is something very special about swimming in the ocean with a bright moon shining above you on your birthday. I swam out about a hundred yards and suddenly realized that there was a very strong rip current. I tried swimming toward the shore, but the harder I swam, the further I was being drawn out. I am usually a fairly strong swimmer, but having consumed too much alcohol, I was getting winded quickly. I prayed for God to help me, and He reminded me to swim north or south and not east to west, and within a few minutes, I reached the shore.

She told me that she was getting concerned for me when she could not see me anymore. I explained that God had His hedge of protection around me, and besides, if He was going to take me, I would be standing in front of Jesus after taking my last earthly breath. She asked me if I truly believed that, and I explained why I did—because of what Jesus said to one of the thieves on the cross. **"And Jesus said to him, 'Assuredly, I say to you, today you will be with me in Paradise'"** (Luke 23:43).

After we left the beach, she drove me back to the bar, and I asked her if I could call her on the weekend to see if she wanted to go to church. She gave me her number which turned out to be bogus, but hopefully, I planted some type of seed, even if I did it while sinning and drinking.

Now realizing that I had too much to drink and not wanting to drive the twenty miles to Kevin and Audrey's, I decided to visit my wife who lived across the street. When she woke up and saw me standing there, I was worried what her reaction would be. Needless to say, we were intimate for the first time in several years, and she later told me happy birthday. God is good.

When I got home the next morning and told Kevin and Audrey what had happened, they looked at me and just shook their heads. They asked me if I told Katie about the girl at the beach. I said of course. They have been married for over thirty-five years and lovingly told me that I have a very strange marriage, which is absolutely true.

I know I am still a carnal sinner at times, but quite honestly, I am looking forward to my next birthday.

Within a month, I woke up during the third watch with a severe stomach pain, and I knew it was the diverticulitis rearing its ugly head. I tried to pray it away, but sometimes the answer is no. Within a few days, I had to go to the hospital, and I called the family to let them know what was going on.

The doctor told me that he wanted me to consider colon resection surgery, which is major surgery. He also said that if I did not address this problem, I may need to have my colon removed and have a colostomy bag. His comments were upsetting, to say the least. I told him that I would have to think and pray about the surgery.

I remained in the hospital for seven days, and this time, they would not even give me clear broth or water. At the risk of sounding self-centered and prideful, I was upset because my three daughters never came to see me, and my two oldest never even called me back. Trust me; I know that people are busy, but Katie worked two jobs and still visited every day.

Kevin and Johnny came one afternoon for a short visit, which I was grateful for, and I was happy to see them. It is very difficult for me to release my concerns to God regarding my children, even though I know that they belong to Him, and I am just their earthly guardian. As I said in the acknowledgment, I am still a work in progress.

When I was released, I continued trying to heal and was physically unable to work. I have never been that active on social media. I only joined Facebook so I could see what my teenagers were posting. I began to realize that I was not taking advantage of this and began posting daily verses from my devotional/journal and hoped that these verses would speak to someone who may need to hear them.

Katie had been talking about going to Michigan for her mother's eightieth birthday because her sisters were planning a big party for her. She asked me if I would stay at the house with the kids if she decided to go. I was very happy that she still cared enough about me to trust me in her house and to watch the kids.

Within a few days, she called to tell me that her sister Judy, who is very generous, had sent everyone airline tickets to Michigan so we would not miss the celebration. For a brief moment, I was very excited until I realized that everyone did not include me. I tried not to take this personally, but my flesh kept telling me that I deserved to go, and quite honestly, I whined about it for the next few weeks.

The only merit to my earthly feelings was that I knew that this might be my last opportunity to see her entire family. Why would I ever have a need to go to Michigan again? I bought her mom a nice birthday card and wrote her a heartfelt message and gave it to Megan the night before they left. The last thing I whispered in her ear was "See you in Michigan." I did not know how I would get there and/ or find the funds, but I had the feeling that I was supposed to go to Michigan. Was this just my selfish flesh feeling neglected, or was my spirit crying out?

I called my brother and sister-in-law, Don and Annette, and asked them if I could stay with them if I decided to make the trip. I had not seen them in over seven years, and they said absolutely. My only problem now was how was I going to get there? I booked a last minute flight which took 80 percent of my paycheck, but if I have learned anything about how our flesh works, it is that we want to do something when everything says we can't.

I arrived in Detroit late Saturday night, and Don picked me up and had a fatty for the ride back to his house. We stayed up late drinking Captain Morgan. He had recently been through the many emotional problems of this world. His father had recently committed suicide, his health was failing, and his youngest son, Justin, had suffered from substance abuse.

Being out of the loop of their daily lives, I was not aware of what was going on. I began to think that my desire to visit Michigan may not have been the selfish flesh but a longing from the Holy Spirit to witness to my extended family.

Although my methods were unorthodox, I did discuss in detail with him what He had done in my life during the last three-plus years. My brother-in-law believes in God but does not like to be preached to, and I could tell that he shuts down when someone tries, so we tried a different approach.

I asked him to ask me questions and concerns that he had about faith, religion, and God. He asked me some of the hardest to explain—why God allows bad things to happen, what happens when we die, is there really a hell, why evil controls our world, etc., etc.

I tried answering his questions with a loving and caring heart, without trying to sound like a legalistic hypocrite, even though I felt like one because we had been carrying on. I tried to explain that it is all about Jesus and our relationship with Him, not about going to church every Sunday and trying to look and act holy.

I have seen my share of well-known pastor's fall, and they usually fall hard. I told him that my words were just that, and actions and attitude should bear good fruit. **"Every tree that does not bear good fruit is cut down and thrown into the fire. Therefore by their fruits you will know them" (Matthew 7:19–20).** I asked him to make his own decision after spending a week with me.

The following evening, we attended the party for my mother-in-law, and even though most of the family was surprised to see me, they were fun to be around. The morning before I left Florida, I felt inspired by the Holy Spirit to do something special for my mother-in-law. I wrote a poem for her and had it printed on religious paper and put in a nice frame. Even though it was written in thirty minutes, I thought it was very special.

The day after the party, I continued talking with my nephew and wanted to get the point across that not everyone is geared to work a typical nine-to-five job. Over the next few days, I think that we bonded because we have a lot in common, and he knows that I have never judged him. It had begun raining early that morning and steadily increased throughout the day.

I called Katie and the kids and asked if they could come by because I wanted to spend time with them before they returned to South Florida. Neither one of us had a vehicle, so she said they would be by later in the day. When they showed up, they were with her mother, her older brother John, and her sister Patty.

I thought they were coming by for a visit, but they wanted to show Megan and I all of the places that they had lived, where they went to school, and the cemetery where her father was buried. Her oldest sister, Annette, also joined us, and the eight of us packed into a minivan, driving through the suburbs of Detroit in the pouring rain. Isn't life grand?

We spent the next several hours driving through several subdivisions, and as we passed dozens of homes that were vacant and for sale, her mother and sister began saying to my wife, "That would be a nice little starter house for you and the kids."

What! Am I invisible? I continued trying to show grace and mercy, but eventually, I had to ask them where would that leave me. They looked at me, smiled, and continued the sightseeing tour.

When we got to the cemetery, it was raining very hard, but they insisted that we get out of the van and pay our respects, which I was happy to do. We said a nice prayer at the grave site, returned to the van, and continued driving when my wife's uncle Bobby popped into my mind.

Fifteen years ago, Katie and I spent an evening in Lexington, Michigan, and ran into her uncle while taking an evening walk. I had always thought that it was strange that we saw him that evening because Katie had not seen him in over a decade, and I had not seen or even thought about him since that night.

After asking about him, Katie's mother told me that he had recently had some health issues but, otherwise, was doing fine. She also said that he has a plot at this cemetery near his brother when he is called home.

When my wife and her family got home, they called Annette to tell us that her uncle Bobby, whom I was just talking about, died this afternoon, just about the time when we were at the cemetery. That began a series of events that I can only explain as just plain weird.

Remember that I said it had been raining all day? Well, one of the small draining canals began to overflow, and the area at Van Dyke and Old Thirteen Mile in Warren, Michigan, was now four to five feet underwater. We walked about a half mile to see what was going on. What I saw amazed me. Vehicles were stuck in the road, and all you could see was the top of the roofs. A woman had just drowned, my nephew saved another man's life, people were stuck in stores and restaurants, and the city had now dispatched boats to rescue those that were unable to leave.

Hundreds of vehicles were ruined, and the footage of the cars stuck on the major highways was something out of a *Falling Skies* scene. We walked back to the house, and I could not help but think how mankind has no control over God's creations, even the weather. My nephew and I stayed up and talked for a few hours.

My older nephew, Jason, was graduating from the Detroit Police Academy later in the week, and I once again, woke up with that awful feeling in my stomach but went to the ceremony anyway. It was held at the Greater Grace Baptist Church in one of the older neighborhoods in Detroit, off of Seven Mile. This is one of the local mega churches and was actually the location where Rosa Park's ceremony was held when she was called home back in 2005. I was very proud of my nephew and would publicly like to ask you to pray for him as he serves in a very rough area in Detroit.

While I was sitting in the church, my stomach problems were getting worse, and I prayed for the healing powers of God the Father through Jesus's stripes. **"But He was wounded for our transgressions, He was bruised for our iniquities; the chastisement for our peace was upon Him, and by His stripes we are healed" (Isaiah 53:5).** This time the answer was yes, and within a few hours, the pain was gone. Thank You, Jesus.

Later that day, we attended the viewing for their uncle, and even though my wife and kids had returned to Florida, I felt that it was the right thing to do. When I saw their aunt, she seemed very nice even though I had never met her and had only seen her husband that one time.

The funeral home was in a beautiful location and the pictures they had displayed were amazing. When Don and I were getting ready to leave, I thanked Katie's aunt, held her hand, and whispered in her ear, "Whoever your God is, and hopefully it is Jesus, may He give you peace and joy this evening when you get home."

Don crashed after we got home, and I was able to spend several hours with Justin talking about a hundred different topics. It was actually nice that it was just the two of us, and we became Facebook friends after I told him that I post a daily verse every day.

I had scheduled an early morning flight from Detroit, and on the way to the airport, Don told me that he did see a change in me and I just seemed happy and my complete attitude was different, which can only be credited to Him and what He was doing with/in/through me. He also thanked me for not preaching to him and respecting his wishes.

Kristy had a healthy baby boy while we were in Michigan, and they named him Asher (happy). And although I had been sad that I missed his birth, I was very happy to see him. I could not help but think that Kristy was upset with me because I missed his birth, but it might just be my insecurity.

For several months, things had continued being very slow at work, and I was forced to work out of town on more than one occasion. I continued to wonder if the lack of work was intentional, hoping that I might seek employment elsewhere. I called an agency based out of Tampa and received a few days of work without being compensated for travel time, gasoline, lodging, or food.

I called my friend Robin, and they were happy to put up with me for a few days. I was forced to terminate work early the second day that I was there, and Robin told me that she attended a Bible study on Wednesday nights. They were currently doing a study on a book called *Crazy Love* written by Francis Chan. She suggested that I read a few of the chapters if I wanted to attend the Bible study with her. I had never heard of him but had nothing else to do.

I have never been so moved by a book (excluding the Bible, of course). I literally could not put it down. I felt that his views and thoughts were as close to mine as I have ever read! There are several topics and quotes that he discusses in his book that I already had in print. Downloading a short video on YouTube for each chapter was genius. I ended up reading half the book that day and have watched several of his videos after getting home.

Within a few days, I headed home and had time to continue to think about this book. I began to wonder if not having any local work and having to break surveillance early because I was chased by a large angry man were predestined so I would read this book. I know that sounds odd, but I somehow (Holy Spirit) knew that I was supposed to read that book at that time.

CHAPTER 14

Pray, Pray, and Pray Again

The lack of work continued throughout November, and I took my last week of vacation during Thanksgiving week. It was on November 27 this year, which was our twenty-first anniversary. Kathleen asked me to spend the day with them, and I was excited when Megan asked me if I would show her how to prepare the turkey and sides for Thanksgiving.

I went by early, and we spent the next several hours getting everything ready. We spent a few hours together talking, and I could not help but think that God was restoring our family and relationships. Megan left in the late afternoon to spend time with her new boyfriend and his parents. I had spoken with Kevin and Renee earlier in the day, and they told me that they were spending the holiday with Kristy. I wished them well.

Within a week, I woke up with the pain of diverticulitis and knew it was the infection and inflammation returning. This started out mild, but by the following morning, it had spread across my abdomen which had never happened before. As they like to say in the hospital, "What is your pain level from 1–10?" Well, it was an 8 or 9. I did not want to return to the ER, but I was concerned about emergency surgery if I waited too long.

Knowing what was ahead of me, I prayed for God to give me the courage and wisdom that I was lacking. Evaluations, vitals, a CAT scan, an IV drip, pain medicine, and admission—you have to love it. I was told that the infection and inflammation were borderline emergency surgery, but they wanted to try a very strong antibiotic to see if it could be controlled. Back to the clear broth, Jell-O, four-hour vital checks, and daily blood work.

On a positive note, this gave me time to write Christmas cards to family and friends. I always feel led to make sure all of my wife's family receives cards with a loving and caring message. Katie is amazing, but Christmas cards are a low priority when you work two jobs.

When I was discharged, the infectious disease doctor told me that she wanted to continue the antibiotics after I was released, but due to the strength of the hospital IV, oral doses would not work. She began talking about something called a PICC line which is a plastic tube inserted into your body, fed to your heart, and requires home health care for two treatments of an IV per day.

This sounded very inconvenient, but considering I could not work, I agreed. Kevin and Audrey were their usual selves, a blessing. After several visits from Michele, my home health care nurse, she was confident that I could do the daily treatments myself, which was weird but more convenient.

Visiting family and friends during the holidays was kind of strange having an IV tube in your arm, but I guess you get used to it. Beats a colostomy bag! I would briefly like to discuss Michelle. She is my age and has an amazing spirit, and we frequently discuss Jesus and the Bible. Out of all of the hundreds of home health care nurses, God chose her to come into my life.

I was still extremely weak and directed my energy to getting healed and tried to appreciate what the future held. Once the infection and inflammation were controlled, I would need another CAT scan, a colonoscopy, and probably the colony resection surgery. I began to realize that it could be weeks if not months before I could return to work. Without any disability insurance or other means of compensation, I was concerned about how I was going to pay my bills.

My financial obligations to my wife, my monthly pledge to Compassion International, and my storage unit were my biggest concerns. Once again, I can tell you from personal experience, we get closer to God when our personal efforts fail, and I prayed for financial favor. I was not thinking large, like the lottery. I just prayed that He would bless me through other people.

I felt the need to return to church, but I wanted and needed a change. I remembered that my friends from the Tuesday night Bible study had told me about a house church that several of them attend, and the message is given by Pastor Bob, my group leader's mentor. Have you ever met someone that is just light-years ahead of you in spiritual knowledge with a way of making the Scriptures come alive?

I had thought about attending this service in the past; I just never got there. The first service I attended was fun, informative, and Spirit filled. They started the service with the 20–25 people singing several praise and worship songs with the lyrics on a large flat screen, and I have to say that it has always been my experience that when the crowd is Spirit filled, the presence of the Lord is larger than life. I have made a group of eternal friends and look forward to seeing them on a regular basis. When I was leaving, one of my friends handed me fifty dollars and said, "God bless you, my brother."

I made arrangements to see my sister-in-law Cheryl and her husband Jim before Christmas and stopped by their house with Megan and Juliette. We visited for a few hours, mostly discussing our battle stories from our recent hospital stays. When we were getting ready to leave, Jim handed me one hundred dollars and told me "God bless!" I knew that He had put this on their hearts because they are also on a fixed/broken income.

I attended our weekly Bible study, and much to my surprise (oh, he of little faith), my brothers in Christ had collected $340 and gave it to me when the meeting started. As grateful as I was, it left me distracted from the Word, and I began thinking about what I could do with the money.

Forgive me if this seems out of line, but most of us are driven by money, whether we realize it or not. If you don't agree with that, go from earning forty thousand a year to nothing. I felt good that I gave Him the praise and glory for answering my prayers.

The following evening was Kevin's second annual Christmas Eve party at their town house. The twins and my wife were working till eight, and I was blessed with the privilege of watching Jules and going to the party with her. I gave the older kids their presents, and they seemed happy when they opened them.

While at the party, I talked with Kristy about getting together on Christmas Day so we could exchange presents at her house. I have to say that watching Kaylani and Jules playing together is one of His greatest blessings. Asher was his happy joyful self.

Having previously missed weeks of Bible study and church due to my health issues, I was unable to organize efforts to do anything for our friends at the park for Christmas morning, which deeply saddened me. I thought about doing something for them before New Year's, but my efforts fell short.

One of things that had brought me great joy was that Johnny had previously began attending my weekly Bible studies with me and had also attended the Sunday church service with me several times, hosted by Pastor Bob and the others. He had opened the door to Christ, even though most of our studies were advanced. He asked honest and sincere questions and told me that he had been running from God but knew that he was supposed to attend with me. I tried to spend as much time with the twins and Juliette and continued messaging the older kids.

I spent the majority of the next two weeks just staying home, reading, and playing Xbox. After a follow up with one of the doctors, she suggested we schedule a CAT scan to determine the outcome once the treatments were completed. One of the good things about really meditating about your life and where the Lord might lead you is that you receive guidance from the Holy Spirit regarding what to do and what not to do.

Still having my financial concerns, I found myself praying more than usual but also found myself praying for personal gain and not praising God for His provisions and love, which I believe to be grace. I had gone several weeks without any money, and once again, God answers prayers.

I was at Megan and Johnny's, and Katie asked me how I was surviving. I told her I was living on a prayer. She then told me that God had put it on her heart to help me and gave me one of her credit cards and told me to use it sparely and just pay her back when I could. This was an incredible act of love because I was already several hundred dollars in arrears to her for my health and auto insurance.

Several days later, the office called to tell me that they had work for me, if I was able to return. I told you prayer works! I really did not have a choice and gladly accepted the assignments, even though I found myself having to administer the IV treatments while sitting in the car, and managed to work four full days. **"I can do all things through Christ who gives me strength" (Philippians 4:13).**

On the first day of work, while driving the hour to the assignment, I was blessed to listen to the *Focus on the Family* radio show with Jim Daley, and he was talking with Dr. Tony Evans about his latest book titled *Raising Kingdom Kids*. I had heard about this book, but his words seem to talk directly to me about my concerns with my family and if I should try to return home.

In early February, I woke up with severe stomach pain and knew the infection had returned. I spent several hours praying and humbly asking Him to remove this problem, but as I said before, sometimes the answer is no. I called Katie and told her what was going on and that I was returning to the hospital. She offered words of encouragement, but I could sense that she was also thinking about the monies owed to her.

As I returned to the hospital routine, I was told that once again, the issues were borderline emergency surgery, but they wanted to try and avoid it because there was a 80 percent chance of needing a colostomy bag. Can you say reality? I had plenty of time to think about my life, my faith, and my God, and found myself thinking about the verse, "My grace is sufficient, My strength is made perfect in your weakness."

After eleven days in the hospital, the swelling and infection were better but still too inflamed to do the surgery. I missed Johnny and Megan's birthday party, although they visited me a few times with Katie and Juliette.

They inserted another PICC line so I could continue the home IV treatments which were now administered by Lucy, a different CNA. Kevin and Audrey continued to be a blessing to me, emotionally and financially, as I continued to heal.

I regularly called my employer, and the office manager always seemed to find humor and joy telling me that there was no work. After a few weeks, I told her if they didn't have any work, I would be forced to file for unemployment compensation. She told me that if I did that, she would give me a four-hour assignment every week which would not allow me to collect benefits. My comment was "I thought you didn't have any work." She laughed and hung up.

This created an enormous amount of stress, and I continued to pray and meditate, knowing that only He could give me the peace and strength that I needed. After hours of prayers and meditation, I dropped off my equipment and a resignation letter and picked up my final check. I did not know what else to do, and as I said before, I really dislike drama and head games. My ex-partner was seldom at work these days because he was recovering from a stroke that occurred in October.

In early March, after another MRI, they determined that the infection was still present and would not perform the colonoscopy but felt that the inflammation was reduced enough to do surgery. They scheduled the colon resection surgery for March 17, 2015, which was three days after Kevin and Jodi's wedding.

When I mentioned traveling out of state to Lucy, I received calls from my three doctors who told me that it was a health risk taking a long trip because of the PICC line and the scheduled surgery. I was also told that they would cancel the scheduled surgery and drop me as a patient if I went against their advice. I told Kevin and the other kids I couldn't attend the wedding. I was happy to see the pictures that they posted on Facebook.

The day before the surgery, I attended a pre-op meeting at the hospital, and although I was grateful that they explained in great detail the surgery and recovery period, I was beginning to get nervous about the seriousness of what was about to happen.

I was not nervous about dying; that I can deal with. **"For to me, to live is Christ, and to die is gain. But if I live on in the flesh, this will mean fruit from my labor; yet what I shall choose I cannot tell. For I am hard pressed between the two, having a desire to depart and be with Christ, which is far better" (Philippians 1:21–**

23). It was the thought of having my colon removed and having to wear a bag for the rest of my life that concerned me. I still haven't gotten use to the dentures!

Katie and the twins called me later that afternoon to talk with me about the surgery and to wish me well and said they would be praying for me. Kevin and Audrey also offered me words of encouragement.

The following morning, I drove myself to the hospital and sat in the car for close to an hour, praying and asking for His hedge of protection. As I was being prepped, I was told by the surgeon that because I had never had the colonoscopy, he would not know how bad the infection was until they saw my colon. He did say that there was a decent chance that my colon would need to be removed. He thought I was joking when I said, "If that's the case, leave me on the table."

When I woke up after the surgery, my beautiful wife was there, which was the good news. The bad news was I had never felt such intense pain and disorientation! Was the surgery successful? Did they remove my colon? When did they insert the catheter? Why won't the nurse answer my questions? I was physically unable to look at my abdomen, and Katie found a mirror so I could see what it looked like.

That was a very surreal moment for me when I looked at the three incisions that were closed with large metal staples. I was later informed by the doctor that the surgery was a success and they removed about eight to nine inches of the infected colon and a bag would not be needed. Thank You, Jesus!

Kathy came to the hospital every day, and Megan, Juliette, and Johnny visited me a few times. On the weekend, Kevin, Kristy, and Renee came to visit after they had gotten home from the wedding.

I remained in the hospital for seven days, and thoughts and concerns about my future continued to overwhelm me. Much to my surprise, I had to continue the home health care routine for several weeks after being released.

These treatments quickly became a problem with mobility due to the IVs having to be administered every 4–5 hours and lasted about an hour. I increased my prayer time and found myself reading the Bible more and more.

After a few weeks, I had to discontinue my donation to Compassion International, which deeply saddened me. I could no longer afford my cell phone and did not have any money for anything. My storage unit payment was in arrears, and I was receiving messages that they would sell my possessions if the bill was not paid. This only added to my stress, and any joy I received was from Jesus.

CHAPTER 15

God Is Good

Easter had come and gone, and although I enjoyed seeing everyone, my health and future continued to concern me. I spent the majority of my time at Kevin and Audrey's but tried to visit the family as much as I could. It is not a good feeling having to coast on the interstate in efforts to conserve gasoline!

My friends from S & L Ministries contacted me and told me when the next breakfast would be held for our friends at the park which brought me joy. I attended the breakfast, and we were told that this would be the last time we could do this because the city had now banned these functions in public areas.

After breakfast, we passed out clothes, blankets, and other items and prayed with our friends and talked about what the city had put into place for their well-being. Matt talked about getting another outreach planned, but as time progressed, we spoke less and less due to that busyness of life thing.

By the summer, I was feeling fine but continued worrying about financial nonsense and not trusting in the Lord. I continued visiting the family when I could, and spending time with Juliette was a lighthouse for me. Thinking about living with them was now a fading thought because I would now be a burden and not an asset.

My good friend from Bible study blessed me financially when he used me as a helper doing pool leak detection. The time I was able to spend with him on a daily basis was just what I needed. Kevin and Audrey continued to be a blessing to me, but no longer paying them regularly to live there burdened my spirit.

My fifty-eighth birthday came and went without much fuss, but Katie and the twins did take me out for dinner. While we were talking, I could tell that Katie was completely exhausted and stressed out over financial matters. I returned home and began thinking and praying about trying to find a steady job. The older kids had sent me a happy birthday text but were unavailable for dinner.

A few weeks later, I stopped into an Italian deli and noticed a hiring sign on the front door. Although I knew that working here would be a fraction of what I was used to earning, I hoped that God would continue to direct my steps. I spoke with the owner who said she would be happy to give me a try. It is difficult to put into words, but I felt as though I was supposed to be here at this time in my life.

Other than spreading the Gospel, preparing and serving food is what I was made for. Fire hot, knives sharp, got it. I found myself sitting in the car each morning before my shift praying for His hedge of protection (because you have to respect the slicer), His peace and joy and asking that I would allow Him to work through me and not of my own accord.

The deli shares the building with a separate produce business, and I began to realize that there were several gay people that worked here, including my boss. Her parents, brother, and partner also worked at the deli.

I began thinking more and more about gays and God and how this gay, lesbian, and transgender thing was going to play out regarding judgment and eternity. I know what the Bible says about being gay, and it's not good, but I also know what it says about love.

I continued thinking about these issues and finally came to the realization that the difference here is grace, the Old Testament versus the New Testament. I truly believe that once you have honestly accepted Jesus, that is the eternal foundation for your glorified body. This is where I think the gender issues end.

I soon realized the enormous blessing that the Father had given me. It was much more than earning money again; it was the ability to talk to others about Christ. I know that this might not sound exciting to most of you, but I had spent the last few decades sitting in a car or an office with the inability to communicate with others without electronic assistance. My boss and I frequently discussed scriptures while working and what God had done in our lives. She openly discussed being gay and seemed to really understand grace and not being judgmental.

Since the deli was located close to the family and twenty miles from Kevin and Audrey's, I began spending more and more time with them and usually stayed over 3–4 nights a week, sleeping on the floor or couch. I tried to be a blessing to Katie and began giving her 40–50 percent of my check while also trying to pay my way at Kevin and Audrey's. This continued for several weeks, and in early July, Katie asked me to bring my things over and stay with them permanently.

I am still amazed at how God works things out when we stop trying to achieve something on our own. He allowed me to slowly return to my family on a trial period to test the waters, so to speak. I was so excited and can honestly say that I prayed and gave Him the thanks for what He was doing in my life.

I hope you know how much I love Kevin and Audrey, but the evening we drove there was somewhat awkward. Allow me to explain. I was on cloud nine because I was officially going to live with my family again after eighteen months. He had healed my physical issues, found me a job, allowed me to discuss Him and His kingdom at work, returned me to my family, and He was restoring my marriage and relationships.

But let's look at it from their perspective. Kevin and Audrey had housed and cared for me when I could barely do it myself. They had cooked hundreds of meals at their own expense, listened to my endless rants about my problems. They had endured me cooking in their kitchen. They had done my laundry and cleaned my sheets and shower more times than I can remember, and all of this without paying them for months at a time. Now that I was earning money regularly, I moved out.

I have tried to keep in close contact with them, but I have His peace and joy knowing that they have received heavenly treasures because they had done what Jesus asked. **"For I was hungry and you gave me food; I was thirsty and you gave me drink; I was a stranger and you took me in"** (Matthew 25:35).

Returning to the family was certainly an adjustment. I had given up a great bedroom and private bath for a sleeping bag and sharing limited space, but I was finally reunited with my family through no efforts of my own. Mercy? I love the way God insists that we have involvement in His decisions.

Within a few weeks, we began attending church as a family on a regular basis, and I truly felt blessed whenever I think about what He has done. This was the church that I attended for a few years and knew most of the members. Katie decided that she wanted to attend the luncheon they were hosting for joining the church, and I attended with her.

We met a nice couple named Tom and Muriel, and God was working through Katie as she discussed our current and past issues, which blew me away because she is a very private and reserved person. We were asked to attend their weekly Bible study group. We attended a few meetings, and I felt so blessed that Katie and I were spending time together again and talking and thinking about the Lord. We are still not a "married couple" by any means, but He is helping us take the first step. Teaching your granddaughter to pray and the stories of the Gospels is another of His awesome blessings.

Things were going well at home and we continued attending church together and I began to see a huge change in Katie, in a positive way. Her budget was now manageable, and her mood and spirit had calmed down, and on occasion, we were somewhat intimate. Like most women, Katie needs a sense of security from her spouse, and although I have been contributing lately, that has not always been the case.

During the end of the summer, my car finally died, but surprisingly, it did not seem to bother me much. I walked the four-and-a-half-mile round-trip distance to and from work for a few weeks until a coworker gave me a bicycle. I actually looked forward to the daily exercise which helped me keep off the weight.

A few weeks before Christmas, I heard that Joyce Meyer was having a speaking engagement at one of the local megachurches in the area. I asked my boss and her partner if they wanted to attend with me, and they agreed. They invited one of their friends, and the four of us really enjoyed her message which was based on the flesh versus the spirit and the importance of not doing what you feel like doing. I should have paid more attention to God's message.

Christmas was awesome, and I felt so blessed to be with my family during these joyful times. Watching small children open Christmas gifts is one of His greatest blessings, at least for me.

Shortly after the new year, I asked my boss what she thought about having a weekly Bible study one night a week after work. She smiled and said that she thought it was a good idea and asked me to let her know what night would be best.

I was very excited about the possibility of having a weekly Bible study with my coworkers since I was no longer attending the Tuesday night study because of watching Juliette when Megan was working. I spent weeks thinking about how to reach different people with different beliefs and wanted to convey the same type of message that Michael, my nephew, had shared with me five years ago. The majority of the anticipated group are people that do not attend church regularly, and God may not be a part of their daily lives.

I decided that the importance of understanding the original sin of mankind and the difference between God's grace and living under the law, was a good place to start. One afternoon, I sat down with my boss and discussed the where and when, and we decided the front patio at the entrance of the business would be a suitable location.

I posted a notice for the Bible study on the business bulletin board, and after a week, I had not heard from anyone. I began wondering if it was the Word of God that they were avoiding or the messenger. I asked my boss why she thought no one was interested. She is very direct and honest, which I like. She told me that my lifestyle doesn't warrant preaching the Gospel and that I seemed like a hypocrite regarding my words and my actions. She also said that "just because you know the Bible, that doesn't mean you should discuss it. How can you smoke and drink on a regular basis and expect to be taken seriously?"

I felt honored that she liked me enough to be completely honest, but I was also haunted by her words. I told her that I could understand how she could think like that, but was it fair that I was not even given a chance?

The Bible study never happened, and I really tried to remind myself about shaking off the dust and moving on, but her views and opinions of me continued to haunt me. Was this my sinful flesh or my spirit trying to help others?

During the next few weeks, I began to find myself being a clock watcher, which I had never done before. My relationship with my coworkers had changed, and I no longer enjoyed being there and battled the thoughts of wanting to quit!

The week after Easter, the entire family had the flu, and I was scheduled to open the deli and slept till noon and never answered my phone. I ended up leaving the deli, and I know that my family was very disappointed in my decision. I spent the next few weeks filling out applications and tried finding work in the food service industry but soon realized that I should have never quit my job, but it was much more than that.

My boss's comments to me regarding being a hypocrite had deeply affected me. I knew I was a child of God and have always tried extending grace to others, but her words made me extremely confused regarding my spiritual life, my identify in Christ, and what I was supposed to be doing or not doing.

Being a Christian and trying to help lead others while trying to do everything right did not seem to work. Hanging out with people that partied and talking about Christ had not worked, and I was viewed as a hypocrite. Whether correct or not, my mindset was that Christ focused on sinners while on earth, not the high priests and holy ones. I guess the difference is that I am a sinner and not the Son of God, kind of a big difference.

I still have more questions than answers, and I believe this is what I have been trying to say throughout the book. It is the flesh versus spirit and the law versus grace, and I repent daily for trying to bring others to Christ while under the influence because I was not a good witness for Him.

I soon realized that my problems were not spiritual because I continued praying and having a close relationship with Him, although I continued battling the flesh. My thoughts and problems were dealing with other people, especially those who call themselves Christians. **"Judge not, that you be not judged. For with what judgment you judge, you will be judged; and with the same measure you use, it will be measured back to you"** (Matthew 7:1–2).

My sister-in-law, Cheryl, who has an awesome relationship with the Lord, has not attended church for several decades because of legalistic churches and people. I had always wondered why she felt this way but began to understand why.

I decided to take a step back with my interaction with others, and being an extremist, I'm sure I concerned several people with my choices. I stopped posting daily Bible verses, secluded myself from my biblical circles and close friends, and found myself thinking more and more about eternity and not the here and now.

I returned to the lifestyle that I lived five years ago when I began my walk with the Lord. I spent the majority of my time with Him and tried to make my family's life a little easier by cooking, cleaning, and organizing and would wait and see how this played out.

Katie and I are still not a "married couple" by any means, but we seldom argue anymore, and we actually enjoy being around each other. I had not seen or spoken with the older kids for months, which continued to burden my spirit. A few days before my birthday, Katie contacted them and hoped to have a party for me with all of them at a local restaurant, the day before my birthday.

Because of everyone's schedule, we were unable to get together, but I was able to speak with the kids, and they wished me a happy birthday. I know that I still have issues with relationships, but as I mentioned before, I am still a work in progress, and the Lord is working overtime on me. I hope you have enjoyed reading some of the stories of my life, but the final chapters have not been written yet.

I humbly ask that you pray for me and my family and the restoration of my relationships. I love the Lord, the body of Christ, and also you. Peace out!

ABOUT THE AUTHOR

Mr. John Benevides has decided to share his personal testimony as he battled through drug addiction and a carnal life, until he stumbled across Jesus Christ. His current release is *Running from Grace, Caught by Mercy*.

He was born in Hartford, Connecticut, in the late fifties and later migrated to South Florida where he continues to live today. John is married and has five adult children and four grandchildren. He was raised learning the Roman Catholic religion and had his communion and confirmation in the church but drifted away when he was very young.

His professional vocation for over thirty years was in the security industry as he worked as a field investigator, office manager, and owner. He often laughs as he confesses that he has had over two hundred jobs during his lifetime.

He enjoys sports and movies, but his passion is the Lord. In the decade since he accepted Christ, he has worked hard to be the hands and feet of Jesus but also continues to struggle with the evils of this earth.

His family and extended family has taught him that there is strength, love, and accountability in family unity. This is also true with the church and our religious community and leaders.

The reader will be given the author's personal email address so questions and fellowship can be shared directly. How can we have a personal testimony without a test?

john_benevides@yahoo.com

CPSIA information can be obtained
at www.ICGtesting.com
Printed in the USA
LVHW030808170222
711257LV00014B/347